FROM
SWING
TO
SOUL

FROM SWING to SOUL

An Illustrated History of
African American Popular Music
from 1930 to 1960

By William Barlow and Cheryl Finley

ELLIOTT & CLARK PUBLISHING
Washington, D.C.

Pictured on cover (clockwise from top left): Duke Ellington, Billie Holiday, Charlie Parker and Dizzy Gillespie, Count Basie, Dinah Washington, The Ink Spots, and Fats Waller.

(Page 2) Fats Waller is pictured here in the 1935 musical, *King of Burlesque*, where he accompanied Alice Faye singing "Spreadin' Rhythm Around" and "I've Got My Fingers Crossed."

(Page 4) Dizzy Gillespie was one of bebop's foremost spokesmen.

Chapter text and biographies by William Barlow
Captions and illustration research by Cheryl Finley
Designed by Gibson Parsons Design
Edited by Elizabeth Brown Lockman
Printed in Hong Kong through Mandarin Offset
5 4 3 2 1   2001 2000 1999 1998 1997 1996 1995 1994

Library of Congress Cataloging-in-Publication Data
Barlow, William, 1943–
    From swing to soul : an illustrated history of African
American popular music from 1930 to 1960 / by William
Barlow and Cheryl Finley.
        p.   cm.
    Includes bibliographical references and index.
    ISBN 1-880216-18-3
    1. Afro-Americans—Music—History and criticism.
2. Popular music—United States—History and criticism.
I. Finley, Cheryl. II. Title.
ML3479 . B37   1994
781 . 64 ' 08996073—dc20   93-40961
                                      CIP
                                      MN

TABLE OF CONTENTS

Introduction
FROM SWING TO SOUL

From 1930 to 1960, African American popular music went through a series of cultural and economic changes that dramatically altered both its soundscape and its commercial potential. Up until World War II, a pattern of black innovation and white popularization dominated the music industry. This pattern was characterized by two complementary historical tendencies. The first was the appropriation of African American song, dance, and humor by white entertainers, which dates back to the heyday of blackface minstrelsy in the antebellum period. The second was the systematic exclusion of African Americans from positions of power within the music industry and its artificial separation of black and white audiences.

This tendency became institutionalized in the 1920s with the emergence of the race-record industry, which relegated popular black music to a separate and unequal marketing structure. As a result, it was only on rare occasions that black music crossed over into the mainstream white pop market. If a popular African American song did happen to make it onto the pop charts, it was as a version covered by a white recording artist.

After World War II, however, a more complex dynamic began to emerge. To be sure, white cover versions of black hit songs persisted well into the 1960s, and, invariably, the imitations sold better than the originals because the pop record market was much larger than the segregated race-record market. But beginning in the 1940s, the reverse was also true; black artists were recording Tin Pan Alley standards in an effort to cross over to the white pop market. By the next decade, they were also crossing over to the pop charts with their own songs.

While this breakthrough greatly increased the commercial potential of African American popular music, it did little to change the economic status quo in the music industry. White businessmen still owned and directed the major record companies and media corporations as well as most of the new independent record labels and local radio stations that sprang up in the 1940s and 1950s. Consequently, they still controlled the production, distribution, and marketing of black popular music—and most of the profits derived from it.

On the cultural side of the equation, the changes came from an entirely different source. African American popular music went through a major generational shift in the 1940s. While the older generation of black musicians continued to favor the swing, jazz, and urban blues styles they had helped to create in the 1920s and 1930s, the younger generation broke with tradition to pioneer two new genres of black music—bebop jazz and rhythm and blues. Once again, the process of African American musical innovation was ignited by a new generation of musical tastes within the black community—as was the case in the 1890s, and to a lesser extent in the 1920s.

The first volume of this series, *From Cakewalks to Concert Halls: An Illustrated History of*

African American Popular Music from 1895 to 1930, chronicles the growth of blues, jazz, and black musical theater during that period. All three of these novel musical genres originated in the 1890s and were nationally prominent by the 1920s. The blues evolved from a rural folk music into a popular urban style known as the vaudeville blues. Jazz began as an urban folk music in New Orleans, migrated north to metropolitan centers, and there developed the popular big-band format that came to the fore-front during the Jazz Age of the 1920s. Black musical theater grew out of African American minstrelsy, flourished for a period of time prior to World War I, then reached its zenith in the 1920s. By the end of the decade, each of these black musical genres had made significant inroads into the entertainment industry, and they were having a sustained impact on American popular culture as a whole.

This second volume, *From Swing to Soul: An Illustrated History of African American Popular Music from 1930 to 1960,* is divided into four parts. The first part, "The Blues Continuum," follows the blues migrations from the rural South to the industrial North during the 1930s and the war years. Part two, "The Jazz Continuum," documents the rise of the swing bands and swing vocalists during the same time period, 1930 to 1945. The third part, "Bebop and the Birth of Modern Jazz," examines the bebop revolution, which during the 1940s transformed jazz into a modern art form, and the music's subsequent push for respectability in the 1950s. The final part, "Rhythm and Blues: Roots and Branches," describes the origins of rhythm and blues in the swing-band jazz, urban blues, and black gospel music of the 1930s and its sudden rise to national prominence in the postwar years. In addition, this section also examines the seminal influence that rhythm and blues had on the birth of rock-'n'-roll in the 1950s. The conclusion to this volume then assesses the emergence of soul music in the 1960s in light of the developments in African American popular music over the previous three decades.

The blues have chronicled everyday life in the 19th and 20th centuries with a power unrivaled by any other musical form. Sung on front porches and street corners, in juke joints and work camps, many blues songs evoke the feelings of hope and despair experienced by generations of disenfranchised African Americans.

etween 1930 and 1945, the blues were transformed from a rural- to an urban-based popular music, setting the stage for the rise of rhythm and blues in the post-war era. During this 15-year span, as the South's rural blues traditions reached their peak in both popularity and influence, these same styles were being radically altered by blues musicians from rural backgrounds who had migrated into the cities.

The major catalyst for this monumental musical shift was the use of electricity. Once the blues musicians acquired the knowledge and the necessary equipment to amplify their voices and instruments, the music started to sound different, and new urban blues styles emerged. As for the rural blues, the practice of electric amplification did not come into use in these circles until after World War II, when amplified musical instruments were already common in cities.

The major rural blues traditions, born as far back as the 1890s, had begun to trickle into southern cities along with rural black migrants after the turn of the century. When they first entered urban milieus, the blues had managed to retain much of their rural sound and flavor. For example, the famous blues-oriented Memphis jug bands, which reached their peak of popularity in the late 1920s and the early 1930s, had more in common with the rural blues string bands of the 1910s than with the urban blues bands of the 1940s. This was because it wasn't until the late 1930s that blues groups in urban centers began to experiment with amplifying their feature instruments, especially the guitar.

The way was cleared for the rise of modern electric blues by the demise of vaudeville blues. The first major urban blues genre, the vaudeville blues reached their height of popularity in the 1920s. During that decade, vaudeville blues divas such as Bessie Smith, Ma Rainey, Mamie Smith, and Ida Cox performed for overflow crowds on the prosperous Theater Owners Booking Association (TOBA) circuit and sold millions of race records to black and white consumers.

At the peak of its influence in the mid-1920s, the TOBA had more than 50 theaters throughout the country affiliated with the enterprise. Well over one million customers a year attended the African American vaudeville shows at these theaters. But competition from radio and talking motion pictures began to cut into the TOBA's audience and profits as early as 1927. Then the Depression delivered the knockout blow, and the TOBA went out of business in 1930. As this left the traveling vaudeville blues troupes without their major source of income, most of them were forced to disband.

The situation in the race-record industry was equally bleak. During the early years of the Depression, the sale of race records fell off an incredible 95 percent, from 110 million in sales in 1927 to 6 million in sales in 1933. Many of the smaller race-record labels went bankrupt or sold out to larger media corporations, while the num-

Arthur "Big Boy" Crudup taught himself to play the guitar around the age of 30. In the 1940s, he appeared with Sonny Boy Williamson on the popular radio program "King Biscuit Time" on KFFA in Helena, Arkansas. Crudup is credited with writing "Greyhound Bus Blues," "Keep Your Hands Off That Woman," and "Rock Me, Mama."

Blues singer Bessie Smith got her first taste of show business while touring in the late teens with a minstrel troupe starring Ma Rainey. The most popular African American recording artist of the post-World War I era, she was accompanied by African American composer and pianist Clarence Williams on her first recording in 1923.

ber of race recordings being produced decreased dramatically.

One of the biggest casualties of this collapse were vaudeville blues releases. By the time the moribund race-record industry was revived in the late 1930s, the vaudeville blues divas were no longer in vogue. They were replaced by a new generation of blues innovators—musicians such as Robert Johnson, Memphis Minnie Douglas, and Aaron "T-Bone" Walker.

The three major rural blues traditions, located in the Mississippi Delta, East Texas, and the Piedmont, all remained viable during the Depression, and in each of these regions, the blues continued to be the secular music of choice among African Americans. The younger blues musicians who came to the forefront in these regions during the 1930s continued to build on the music of their mentors. But many of these younger musicians also visited the urban blues centers; and as this traffic increased, so did the exchange of styles and techniques between the rural and urban poles of the blues continuum.

The Mississippi Delta changed very little during the first four decades of the 20th century.

At the onset of World War II, the region was still a backward and rigidly segregated agricultural society dominated by a small group of wealthy white cotton planters and merchants. The Delta's black population, which outnumbered the region's white population by more than three to one, remained economically dependent on their white employers and landlords. They were still denied their basic civil rights, subjected to political disenfranchisement, and confined to the social order's lowest stratum.

African Americans in the region had little access to public education or health care, and their living conditions were crude and often unsanitary. The housing they were assigned lacked plumbing and electricity; their diets lacked nourishing foods. From 1930 to 1945, the death and disease rates for the Delta's black residents were much higher than those of their white counterparts, as had been the case ever since the end of slavery.

The cotton plantations continued to be the major source of employment for black workers in the Delta. On these plantations, as in the past, sharecropping and tenant farming dominated the economic arrangements. However, the region was just as infamous for its levee contract labor system.

The levees along the Mississippi River and its tributaries were the only line of defense against the periodic floods that imperiled the entire river basin. The flooding was especially problematic in the Delta, where swamplands had been cleared and drained to make room for the cotton fields. When the river overflowed, it turned much of the region into a shallow lake, which in some places was 50 miles wide.

The earliest levees were built before the Civil War by slave labor; they were then maintained and expanded by convict labor in the postbellum era. After the turn of the century, the federal government became responsible for maintaining the levees, and it phased out the convict labor system only to replace it with another system that proved to be just as invidious. When convict labor was forbidden on the levees, the local white labor contractors now charged with supervising the work hired African American laborers. To billet the workers, they set up a network of levee camps near the work sites. Discipline was enforced by armed guards both on the job and in the camps. In addition, the black laborers were charged exorbitant fees for their food, clothing, shelter, and recreation. As a result, they usually owed the contractors more than they were getting paid.

This system of peonage was remarkably similar to the system already in place on the Delta's cotton plantations. In both cases, African American workers were required to perform backbreaking labor from sunup to sundown, live in overpriced and substandard housing, and purchase all their worldly goods from their employers, to whom they were perpetually in debt.

During the 1930s, there were about 50 federally funded levee camps in the Mississippi Delta;

on the average, about 300 workers were employed at each site. These camps were so notorious that early in the decade the NAACP sent a delegation to investigate the living and working conditions in them firsthand. The leader of this investigation reported back that wages were as low as one dollar a day, workers regularly worked from 12 to 16 hours a day, and discipline was harsh and often brutal. Furthermore, the workers' living quarters were unsanitary, they were often cheated in their pay arrangements, and the goods sold in the camp commissaries were grossly overpriced. The NAACP presented this information to the federal government and asked that it look into the abuses taking place in the camps, but the pleas fell on deaf ears, even within the liberal Roosevelt Administration.

Such titles as "The Boll Weevil," "Old Cotton Fields at Home," and "Pick a Bale of Cotton," as well as the lyrics of many early blues songs of the Mississippi Delta, reflect the harsh working conditions endured by the field hands, sharecroppers, and day laborers who composed them.

The levee camp program, funded by federal monies, remained intact until after World War II.

Most of the levee camps in the Delta had their own juke joints for drinking and gambling. These establishments, like everything else in the camps, were run by the white contractors. The jukes often featured live music on weekends, and many of them even provided an upright house piano. Delta blues musicians, especially pianists such as Sunnyland Slim, Memphis Slim, and Roosevelt Sykes, regularly visited the levee camps to entertain the black workers. A number of these musicians, including Big Bill Broonzy, Big Joe Williams, and Sunnyland Slim, also worked as laborers on the levees. Consequently, popular folk blues such

as "Levee Camp Blues," "Levee Camp Moan," and "Shack Bully Stomp" became favorites throughout the region.

During the 1930s, a younger generation of blues musicians began to emerge as popular figures in the Delta; among the more prominent were Robert Johnson, Rice Miller, Sunnyland Slim, Muddy Waters, and Howlin' Wolf. Collectively, this group infused the music with a new sense of urgency and vitality. Not only were they influential in their own region, but their fame and music began to spread beyond the Delta—and not accidentally. By the end of the decade, a large-scale African American exodus from the region was in the making, spurred on by both the ongoing Depression and the economic dynamics of the plantation system.

Sharecropping and its variations all led to a cycle of debt and dependence for members of the black agricultural work force; very few of them were able to save enough money to purchase their own land. A sociological study of the Delta in the early 1930s revealed that fewer than 20 percent of the indigenous black field hands made a profit from their labors and more than 70 percent were routinely cheated by their landlords. On the average, black families moved from plantation to plantation every other year. It was a common joke among African Americans living on the plantations that the only way to get out of debt in the Delta was to "walk out." During the Depression, that's exactly what many of them started to do, and the

The juke joints of the rural South featured live blues and dancing and catered to a working class. Typically constructed of unfinished plank walls and roofed with tin, they were usually open late at night and on weekends, when patrons were most likely to have spending money.

African American population in the region began to slowly decline for the first time ever.

The advent of World War II accelerated this exodus: now there was the added pull of better-paying jobs in the military and the defense industries. Not surprisingly, Delta blues musicians were a part of this migration. Muddy Waters, Howlin' Wolf, Rice Miller, Sunnyland Slim, Bukka White, Big Boy Crudup, John Lee Hooker, and B. B. King, along with legions more who did not become as well known, all left the region during the 1930s and early 1940s. They were eventually responsible for focusing national attention on the Delta blues style and repertoire, as well as for incorporating the music into the emerging modern electric blues.

The social conditions that gave rise to an East Texas blues tradition were similar to those in the Delta. The region had experienced a large influx of slave labor just prior to the Civil War. Then in the aftermath of the conflict, East Texas, like other cotton-belt enclaves, continued to maintain much of the antebellum plantation economy through sharecropping and tenant farming.

In the 1880s and 1890s, the state established a string of prison farms along the Trinity and Brazos rivers. Even though African Americans made up only 25 percent of the population in Texas, the large majority of the inmates assigned to these penal institutions were black. The living and working conditions on these farms were notorious for their severity, and the prison wardens routinely leased out convict labor gangs to the white

planters who owned the nearby cotton and sugar plantations. This practice, along with the harsh prison conditions, remained intact until well into the 1940s.

The infamous East Texas prison farms were indirectly responsible for the survival of a rural work song tradition in the region, and by extension, a rural blues tradition. The continued use of gang labor in the cane and cotton fields allowed the work song to remain functional in prison farm work and life. The call-and-response patterns in the music supplied the rhythms for the backbreaking labor, while the folk lyrics documented the convicts' feelings and registered their defiance, most often covert, of the institutions and individuals in control of their lives.

Buddy Moss is seen here playing guitar for fellow inmates in a Greene County, Georgia, prison in 1941. Along with rural field hands and mill workers, convicts on penitentiary chain gangs were responsible for creating the blues, and the lyrics often speak of the hardships they faced serving time.

Although work songs were sung on penal farms throughout the South, they were especially prominent in East Texas, where they were an essential component of a common blues repertoire. Much of the folklore associated with East Texas work songs found its way into the local blues tradition. Folk songs such as "Ain't No More Cane on the Brazos," "Don't Ease Me In," "Midnight Special," "Shorty George," and "Two White Horses Standing in Line" were part of a repertoire shared by the region's blues musicians, many of whom served time on the East Texas prison farms.

By the 1930s, a number of the pioneering East Texas blues musicians had passed from the scene. Blind Lemon Jefferson died in Chicago in 1929; Henry "Ragtime Texas" Thomas dropped out of sight about the same time; Huddie "Leadbelly" Ledbetter was on a penal farm in Louisiana in the early 1930s and then was based in New York City for the rest of the decade.

These pioneers were replaced by a new generation of East Texas blues musicians, the most prominent being vocalist Texas Alexander; guitarists Sam "Lightnin'" Hopkins, Clarence "Gatemouth" Brown, Lowell Fulsom, and Aaron "T-Bone" Walker; pianists Ivory Joe Hunter, Joe Liggins, and Charles Brown; and saxophonists Buster Smith and Arnett Cobb. They collectively helped to shape the region's blues into a taut, dance-oriented ensemble music highlighted by rolling piano accompaniments, riffing horns, and innovative single-string guitar solos. (Both Alexander and Hopkins were also incarcerated on local prison farms and worked as convict laborers during this period, and Alexander's repertoire included two well-known prison blues, "They Accused Me of Murder" and "Section Gang Blues.")

By the end of the decade, most of these musicians joined the African

Legendary folk and blues figure Huddie "Leadbelly" Ledbetter had been singing and playing guitar and harmonica for years, but his big break as a musician came ironically when he was serving a term for attempted homicide in Louisiana State Penitentiary, where folklorist John A. Lomax, Sr., first recorded him for the Library of Congress in 1933.

American migration into the military service or into the cities to work in the war industries. Lowell Fulsom joined the Navy, and Lightnin' Hopkins and Gatemouth Brown settled in Houston, while T-Bone Walker, Charles Brown, Joe Liggins, and Ivory Joe Hunter migrated to Los Angeles. All would be in the forefront of the development of modern electric blues in the post-World War II era.

The Piedmont farmlands stretch from Georgia north through the Carolinas and into southern Virginia. After the Civil War, the rural black population in this region continued to labor in the cotton and tobacco fields as tenant farmers and sharecroppers, much like their Delta and East Texas counterparts. The difference, however, was that the agricultural lands in the Southeast had been in use much longer, and the monocrop approach to farming began to cause serious soil depletion as early as the Reconstruction era.

This not only cut into the profits of the cotton and tobacco planters—and by extension, the earnings of their black employees—but it also drove most of the region's small, independent white farmers into bankruptcy. Many of them were later employed in the new Piedmont cotton mills, built around the turn of the century to provide the "New South" with its own industrial base and to provide white workers with jobs. This development helped to solidify racial segregation both in the work force and the society at large. It wasn't until the Civil Rights movement of the 1960s that race relations in the region began to change dramatically.

Blind Willie McTell was taught the guitar by his mother when he was a teen. Also an accomplished accordion, harmonica, and violin player, he began his recording career in 1927 on the Victor label in Atlanta. By 1940, his music had been recorded in one of the famous Library of Congress field sessions.

The rural blues tradition in the Piedmont sprang up after the turn of the century and reached its peak in the 1930s, when the first generation of African Americans who grew up with the blues came of age. Foremost among these young musicians were Blind Willie McTell, Blind Boy Fuller, Sonny Terry, Gary Davis, and Josh White. Some of the most popular songs associated with this group were "Red River Blues," which referred to the region's red clay soil that turned the local rivers a similar color; "Pickin' Low Cotton," which alluded to the small cotton plants grown in the Piedmont due to the soil depletion; "Statesboro Blues," which cited the rural Georgia hometown of Blind Willie McTell, the author of the song; and "Rag Mama Rag," which referred to the ragtime-influenced

guitar style that was at the center of the Piedmont blues tradition.

By the end of World War II, African American migration from the Piedmont into the urban centers along the Eastern Seaboard had reached an all-time high. Many of the region's most talented blues musicians joined this exodus. But unlike the rural blues from the Delta and East Texas, the Piedmont variety did not fare well in an urban milieu. The region's lilting blues melodies and its delicate finger-picking guitar style were not greatly enhanced by amplification; nor were the guitar and harmonica duos, which were another trademark of the tradition. The Piedmont blues would remain an important cultural component of the depleted black farming communities in the region, but they would never make a major impact on the new

urban blues styles emerging during the postwar era.

When the blues reached the cities in the South and then the North, they came under the influence of two disparate cultural forces: the music industry and the ghetto tenderloins, also known as red-light districts. Both of these urban phenomena had contradictory effects on the blues—effects that dramatically transformed their soundscape and lyrical content. The music industry introduced blues recordings to a nationwide black audience, as well as to a more select white audience. In the process, it documented some of this new folk music for posterity. On the downside, it also attempted to standardize the blues form, trivialize its contents, and financially exploit blues artists. The red-light districts likewise had a paradoxical influence on the music. The underworld economies at the heart of these tenderloins provided blues musicians with jobs playing their own music, which in turn gave them the social and physical space to experiment with their art among their peers. In addition, the red-light districts infused the blues with the restless and rebellious ethos of the resident black underclass.

But the decadence, violence, crime, vice, alcohol and drug addiction, disease, and poverty endemic to the ghetto tenderloins eventually took their toll on blues musicians, like everyone else. As a consequence, many of the most talented urban blues artists of the first half of the 20th century never got a chance to record their own music or to reach their full potential due to their premature deterioration or death. Ultimately, all of these contradictions came into play in the rise of urban blues.

Show business proved to be the high road for the blues migrations into the cities. Prior to the Depression, the TOBA circuit, the black musical revues, and the race-record industry were all thriving commercial enterprises. But with the onset of the 1930s, all three entities went out of business—two of them permanently. Only the race-record industry managed to make a comeback later in the decade when the New Deal breathed new life into the stagnant economy. The repeal of Prohibition in 1933 slowly revitalized the nightclubs and saloons in urban America. Simultaneously, the demand for popular records was stimulated by a new technological innovation, the jukebox, which began to supplant live music in the bars and clubs.

Although the curtailment of live performances tended to hurt black professional musicians, it was a boon for the record manufacturers; their business picked up considerably with the spread of the jukebox. Record sales rebounded in the mid-1930s, and the few surviving race-record labels began to replenish the marketplace with new blues releases. At this juncture, the major emphasis was on recording rural blues performers and the newly emerging urban blues bands. However, the industry's policy of segregated labels and markets remained intact, and the Chicago *Defender* and a few other black urban newspapers continued to be the major conduit of advertising for the race-record labels.

The most important race-record producer in the 1930s and 1940s was Lester Melrose, a white native of Illinois who, along with his brother, ran a music store and publishing company in Chicago during the 1920s. In 1934, he was hired as the local manager for RCA Victor's new race label, Bluebird. Melrose had published compositions by Jelly Roll Morton and Joe "King" Oliver; he was familiar with African American musicians in Chicago and had a good ear for their music. For almost two decades, he dominated the race-record operations in the city through his exclusive arrangements with RCA Victor and then Columbia Records. By his own estimate, he was responsible for 90 percent of the blues recorded on these labels from 1934 to 1950.

Melrose's mode of operation was similar to that of Mayo "Ink" Williams, Chicago's biggest race-record producer in the 1920s. Like Williams, he selected a close-knit group of local black musicians and tunesmiths to back up any outside talent he brought into the studio. This group was a virtual who's who of Chicago blues musicians

This wide-eyed, grinning, blackface caricature was typical of the advertising used to promote "race" recordings through the end of the 1930s. In the era before the Great Depression, even some companies owned and run by African Americans employed such stereotypes to sell their music.

during the Depression and the war years. It included female vocalists Victoria Spivey and Lil Green; pianists Blind John Davis, Black Bob, Little Brother Montgomery, Roosevelt Sykes, Walter Davis, Josh Altheimer, Memphis Slim, and Major "Big Maceo" Merriweather; harmonica players Jazz Gillum and Sonny Boy Williamson; guitarists Lonnie Johnson, Big Bill Broonzy, Tampa Red, Amos Eaton aka "Bumble Bee Slim," Johnny Temple, and Memphis Minnie Douglas; bass players Ransome Knowling, Alfred Elkins, Bill Settles, and a youthful Willie Dixon. The studio drummer was usually Fred Williams. The stable of songwriters included Robert Brown aka "Washboard Sam," Big Bill Broonzy, Bumble Bee Slim, Tampa Red, Memphis Slim, Sonny Boy Williamson, and Memphis Minnie. In addition, Melrose recorded a number of rural blues musicians during this period; the most successful were Bukka White, Big Joe Williams, Tommy McClennan, and Arthur "Big Boy" Crudup.

The Bluebird label was soon challenged in the race-record market by Decca, which was launched in Chicago and New York late in 1935 under the direction of Jack Kapp, a crafty veteran of the recording business. He hired Ink Williams as his chief black talent scout, who in turn hired a studio band to back up the local blues artists they contracted. The band was known as the Harlem Hamfats; it included Johnny Temple, Frankie "Half Pint" Jackson, and vocalist Rosetta Howard. Over the next seven years, Decca recorded the rural blues of Kokomo Arnold, Blind Boy Fuller, and Sleepy John Estes, as well as the city blues of Peetie Wheatstraw and Louis Jordan.

In 1938, CBS bought the ailing Columbia record label and launched a talent raid on RCA Victor and Decca. Under John Hammond, a freelance record producer for the Columbia label based in New York City, Columbia signed up the Count Basie and Benny Goodman bands. Hammond had supervised Bessie Smith's last sessions for the label in 1933, and during his early career with Columbia he was able to also sign and record some of the most important blues and jazz musicians of the era: Fletcher Henderson, Duke Ellington, Coleman Hawkins, Albert Ammons, Meade Lux Lewis, Teddy Wilson, Charlie Christian, Ida Cox, and Billie Holiday.

Bassist Willie Dixon and pianist Memphis Slim shared a long musical association that nationally promoted the urban blues tradition through radio programs, recordings, and performances. They first recorded together in 1947, when Dixon joined Memphis Slim and His House Rockers for a session in Chicago on the Miracle label.

The ghetto tenderloins proved to be the low road for blues migrations into the cities. The emergence of these red-light districts coincided with the accelerated growth of industrialism in the nation's burgeoning urban centers in the late 1800s and early 1900s, when the rapid influx of immigrant and migrant laborers seeking work in the new industries changed the cities' landscape. Overcrowded ethnic ghettos gave birth to local ward political organizations; they delivered the ethnic vote to city hall in exchange for patronage.

These organizations became the backbone of urban political machines, which gained control over the political and economic life of key industrial cities. The machines not only doled out patronage to their ethnic constituencies (Irish, Polish, Italians, African Americans, and others); for a share of the profits, they also sanctioned the underworld vice operations—gambling, prostitution, illegal drugs, and alcohol—that flourished in the ghetto tenderloins.

A number of the urban blues centers in the South featured their own unique brand of early urban blues, the most prominent being New Orleans, Atlanta, Birmingham, Dallas, and Houston. But the southern city that had perhaps the most profound influence on the development of urban blues in their formative years was Memphis, Tennessee.

Like New Orleans, Memphis was a bustling,

Will Shade formed the Memphis Jug Band in 1924. The group, which included at various times Ben Ramey, Will Weldon, Charlie Burse, Furry Lewis, Jab Jones, Memphis Minnie, and Charlie Pierce, recorded more than 70 sides. Shade played the guitar, harmonica, jug, and tub or "streamline" bass, with which he is pictured here in Memphis in 1960.

river-port, trade, transportation, and manufacturing center, with a tenderloin haven for pleasure seekers and for talented black musicians. The city's political machine was lorded over by Edward "Boss" Crump, a wily segregationist politician who garnered the local black vote in exchange for patronage and the sanctioning of a wide-open tenderloin nightlife on Beale Street. Cocaine use was rampant in the red-light district, as was the consumption of illegal liquor during the Prohibition era. Moreover, Beale Street became a magnet for Delta blues performers, as well as for rural blues musicians from the surrounding Tennessee and Arkansas countryside.

In the 1930s, the city was base for a number of influential jug bands that played a rudimentary but lively brand of urban blues. These bands used guitars, banjos, harmonicas, kazoos, and whiskey jugs. The most popular were Gus Cannon's Jug Stompers, featuring the legendary Noah Lewis on harmonica, and the Memphis Jug Band, featuring Will Shade on harmonica and Laughing Charley Burse on guitar and vocals. Burse's suggestive, hip-shaking routine and his use of his guitar as a phallic symbol would be imitated much later in his career by an impressionable young white guitarist and singer named Elvis Presley. These borrowed stage antics helped to launch Presley's career as a rock-'n'-roll star. Other important Memphis-based blues musicians active in the 1930s were guitarists Furry Lewis, Frank Stokes, and Memphis Minnie Douglas; pianists Jab Jones and Memphis

Early street musicians, like those shown here with an accordion and washboard, used a variety of common household utensils, gadgets, and automobile parts to make their music. Old bottles, rubber tire tubes, cigar boxes, metal pipes, and stoneware jugs took on new life in the hands of these inventive performers.

Slim; harmonica players Hamie Nixon, Big Walter Horton, and John Lee "Sonny Boy" Williamson; and Sleepy John Estes, the group's most talented blues composer.

During the 1940s, Memphis continued to be a hub of blues activity, although Boss Crump's political machine was finally dismantled and Beale Street went into a decline. Urban blues artists such as Howlin' Wolf, B. B. King, Bobby Blue Bland, Junior Parker, and James Cotton all cut their teeth on the Memphis blues scene before moving on. In the case of B. B. King, this involved becoming the nation's premiere electric blues guitarist and ultimately an international symbol of the music.

During the Depression and the war years, there were numerous urban blues hotbeds in the Midwest, including St. Louis, Indianapolis, Cincinnati, Detroit, and Kansas City. However, it was Chicago that became the mecca of urban blues,

Riley "Blues Boy" King has been one of the leading blues singer-guitarists since the mid-1950s. Local recognition received for a 10-minute deejay spot on WDIA radio in Memphis led to his first big break in the music industry. His most popular hit, "The Thrill Is Gone," was released in December 1969.

both in the Midwest and throughout the country. The city was not only the locale of a well-established black ghetto, overflowing with migrants from the Mississippi Delta, it was also the site of a large race-record operation, second only to New York in size and influence.

The massive influx of rural African Americans had begun in earnest during World War I, when the Chicago *Defender* launched its "Great Northern Drive" to bring southern black migrants to the city. At the onset of the 1930s, Chicago's Southside ghetto had more African Americans living there than any other urban center, with the exception of Harlem in New York City. During the Depression, boogie-woogie pianists such as

Albert Ammons and Meade Lux Lewis came to the forefront of the Southside blues scene. In addition, the pioneering urban blues bands, such as those organized by Sonny Boy Williamson and Memphis Slim, began to transform the traditional Delta blues into the forceful ensemble dance music that would characterize modern Chicago blues.

Sonny Boy's band featured his harmonica and electric guitar, a rhythm guitar, then a bass, and eventually drums and piano. It was a prototype of what would follow in the postwar era, which proved to be the golden age of Chicago blues. The bands of Muddy Waters and Howlin' Wolf, along with their recordings on Chess Records, not only set the tone and style of postwar Chicago blues, but also influenced the future course of black popular music in the United States for years to come.

The West Coast was the final haven for the urban blues tradition. California attracted many African Americans from Texas and the Southwest during the black urban migrations, and the state's African American population reached the half-million mark during World War II. Most of the black migrants settled in Los Angeles or the San Francisco Bay Area, where they worked in the oil refineries and the shipyards.

In the 1930s and 1940s, Los Angeles was the major blues hotspot on the West Coast. Blues musicians played in the bars and nightclubs along Central Avenue in the Watts ghetto, and some were lucky enough to eventually be recorded by the small independent labels that sprang up in the city after the war. The best-known blues artists based in Los Angeles during this period were Cecil Grant, Charles Brown, Joe Liggins, Ivory Joe Hunter, Amos Milburn, and Mel Walker, all of whom played piano and wrote their own songs. The other important blues musicians residing there included vocalists Roy Milton and Wynonie Harris, as well as guitar virtuoso T-Bone Walker, who pioneered the use of the electric guitar in his blues bands at nightclubs along Central Avenue in the late 1930s. Farther north in the San Francisco Bay Area, the best-known blues musicians were guitarist Lowell Fulsom and pianist Jimmy McCracklin.

Yet even as the golden age of urban blues was cresting in Chicago and on the West Coast, it was being supplanted by a new black musical form called "rhythm and blues," especially among African American youth. This generational challenge triggered a diffusion of modern urban blues into the newly emerging musical trends, both black and white, that came to the forefront in the postwar era. Not only can urban blues influences be found in black rhythm and blues, soul, and eventually rap musical styles, they are also present in white rock-'n'-roll and all subsequent rock music styles.

In addition to this diffusion of urban blues into much of American popular music, the blues tradition has also played an important historical role in articulating and spreading African American cultural resistance to white domination in the society as a whole. Blues texts were working-class discourses on American society as seen from the bottom up. Blues performances were collective healing rituals involving audience and artists in a self-affirming catharsis that purged the despair and pain of the past and present. And blues artists have always been cultural rebels, their music and their lifestyles implicitly questioning their second-class status in the white-controlled social order. These characteristics would have a subversive influence on popular American music, black and white, for years to come.

The Club Alabam was a famed local nightclub on Los Angeles' Central Avenue in the 1930s and 1940s. A club of the same name was popular in Harlem in the late 1920s. From the 1920s through the 1940s, jazz clubs across the country often borrowed the names of successful New York clubs to boost their own reputations.

ROBERT JOHNSON

Robert Johnson is a seminal figure in both blues history and blues mythology. In his life and his style of playing, he was one of the first blues performers from the Mississippi Delta to bridge the gap between the music's rural roots and its urban fruits. Unfortunately, however, Johnson died before receiving any widespread recognition for his pioneering musical innovations and accomplishments; and ironically, his early demise inadvertently contributed to the myths and fables about his life that have proliferated since his death in 1938. Over the years, the legend of Robert Johnson has tended to obscure his musical legacy. His canonization as a rock-'n'-roll cult figure has far overshadowed the pivotal role he played in the migration of the blues from a rural to an urban culture.

Robert Johnson was born in the southern Mississippi town of Hazelhurst on May 8, 1911. He was raised by his mother, Julia Dodds, who, for a short time, worked as a migrant field hand. He may never have known his father, Noah Johnson, whose association with Julia Dodds had been brief. Before young Robert reached the age of eight, he had moved with his mother from Hazelhurst up north into the Delta, then on to Memphis for a couple of years, and back to the Delta.

The rest of his youth was spent at a sharecroppers' settlement called Commerce, on a large plantation near Robinsonville, Mississippi. There Johnson went to work in the cotton fields, and at the age of 17, married his 15-year-old sweetheart. A year later she died in childbirth, along with their child.

After this loss, Robert Johnson became restless and never really settled down again. He left Robinsonville for a life on the road as an itinerant blues musician. For the next eight years, he was constantly on the move, spending time in Helena, Arkansas; Memphis, Tennessee; St. Louis, Missouri; Chicago, Illinois; Detroit, Michigan; New York, New York; and Dallas and San Antonio, Texas. During these sojourns, he teamed up with other musicians for short stretches of time, mostly fellow Delta bluesmen such as Rice Miller aka "Sonny Boy Williamson," Honey Boy Edwards, Houston Stackhouse, Willie Brown, and Johnny Shines. In spite of his many musical partners, Johnson remained a loner and something of an enigma even to those who knew him.

Robert Johnson is often remembered as a spellbinding performer on stage and an incorrigible ladies' man off stage. He was boyishly handsome, slight of build, and always well dressed. After the death of his first wife, he took up with a succession of female companions and married at least one of them in the process, but he never stayed long with any of his lovers.

In many respects, Johnson's restless and mercurial lifestyle was symbolic of the changes taking place among the rural black population still working and living in the South's cotton belt in the 1930s. The Great Depression was the final deathblow to the already declining cotton economy; the agricultural work force was uprooted and had to move elsewhere in search of employment.

Johnson was no different from most, other than the fact that he made his living as a musician.

Like many others of his background and generation, he was drawn to the urban centers where jobs were more plentiful for both workers and musicians, but unlike most of the other migrants, he always returned to his home base in the Mississippi Delta. It was there at a juke joint near the town of Greenwood that Robert Johnson was poisoned by a jealous husband. He died a few days later, on August 16, 1938, at the age of 27.

Johnson had little formal schooling and could not read music, but he could remember any kind of music he heard and play or sing it back note for note. His schooling in the Delta blues tradition took place while he was still a teenager, at the weekend dances and parties around Robinsonville. It was there that he met Charley Patton, Willie Brown, and Son House, who introduced him to the guitar. Up to that point, he was playing a harmonica, but soon the guitar became his instrument of choice. He was especially fascinated by Son House's bottleneck slide technique, which he made the centerpiece of his own playing style.

However, Robert Johnson's musical tastes

This is one of only three surviving photographs of Robert Johnson, taken when he was about 24. It is a studio portrait by the Memphis-based Hooks Brothers, African American photographers who from about 1910 through 1985 captured the likenesses of many blues luminaries who passed through that city.

ventured far beyond the sounds of the Delta blues. He listened with great interest to a wide variety of genres—gospel, jazz, country-and-western, Tex-Mex, Tin Pan Alley—and incorporated them into both his style and repertoire. His guitar playing was also influenced by the race recordings of early urban blues guitarists such as Kokomo Arnold, Scrapper Blackwell, and Lonnie Johnson, while his vocal style drew upon urban blues vocal pioneers such as Peetie Wheatstraw and Leroy Carr, as well as the famous cowboy singer Jimmie Rodgers. This eclecticism became the basis for his innovative guitar playing and vocal styling.

The only recordings of Robert Johnson were made in Texas during sessions held in San Antonio in November 1936, and Dallas in June 1937. He recorded a total of 29 songs during these two dates. The record producer on Johnson's recording sessions for the Vocalion label in San Antonio was Don Law; he was impressed with the young musician's dexterity with a guitar, and with his "beautiful hands." While in San Antonio, Johnson was arrested for vagrancy and taken to jail, where he was beaten by the police and his guitar was broken. Don Law bailed him out so that he could complete the recording sessions taking place in a local hotel.

The recordings were all blues songs; either they were Robert Johnson's own compositions, or they were numbers he borrowed from other sources. In the latter category are songs such as "Walkin' Blues," a tune that borrows its melody from Son House's "My Black Mama," "Sweet Home Chicago," based on Kokomo Arnold's "Original Kokomo Blues," and "32-20 Blues," a copy of Skip James' "20-20 Blues." During this period, it was common practice for blues musicians to cover songs recorded by other musicians without crediting them for the compositions; usually, this involved rearranging the song to give it their own personal touch.

It was Robert Johnson's original blues compositions, however, that proved to be his most popular and enduring recordings. While the melodies on these records are fairly predictable because they are based on about five song families, the lyrics are striking for their poetic imagery and their unsettling themes.

In his lyrics, Johnson is often preoccupied with the complexities of love, and he covers the entire range of human emotions associated with the battle of the sexes. Somber blues ballads of unrequited love, such as the haunting "Love in Vain Blues," are juxtaposed with saucy celebrations of erotic love, such as "Travelling Riverside Blues," which includes the line, "You can squeeze my lemon 'til the juice runs down my ... leg." His most popular song, "Terraplane Blues," uses the metaphor of a prized automobile engine to boast of his prowess as a lover.

On the other hand, some of Johnson's blues compositions also allude to social themes and images representative of those found in the early rural blues of the Delta and throughout the Cotton

Belt. In songs such as "Walkin' Blues," "Ramblin' on My Mind," "I Believe I'll Dust My Broom," and "Sweet Home Chicago," he uses the imagery of social mobility as a metaphor for personal freedom.

In tandem with this obsession with freedom and mobility is Johnson's fatalistic assessment of the social and supernatural forces arrayed against him. He expresses this fatalism most eloquently in songs such as "Hellhound on My Trail" and "Cross Road Blues." The latter composition simultaneously evokes the terror of the Delta social order as experienced by an African American citizen at sundown, when the local curfew went into effect, and the spirit of the Yoruba god of the crossroads, the trickster Legba. In Yoruban folklore, a crossroads symbolizes the junction between the physical and spiritual worlds, the human and divine, where members of the tribe seek out the god Legba to learn about their fate in this world and the next. It is no accident that Legba is often associated with the Satan of Christianity in African American folklore.

In many respects, Robert Johnson's flirtation with the supernatural forces of evil, as exemplified in his "Me and the Devil Blues," was an extension of the fatalism implicit in his philosophy of life. Like other blues pioneers, he encouraged the myth that he made a secret pact with the Devil at the crossroads, selling his soul in return for his musical talents. And in the end, the celebrity status as a blues legend that his talents earned

him, as well as his attraction to women, led to his early demise.

Johnson's vocal, and especially his guitar, stylings proved to be as influential as his blues compositions. Lacking the strong voice needed to sing the "deep blues" of Delta greats Charley Patton and later Muddy Waters, he went to the opposite extreme by concentrating on singing in falsetto, as had the Texas blues bard Blind Lemon Jefferson and Skip James, who also hailed from rural Mississippi. The tone and pitch of Robert Johnson's voice gave it both a sweet and a bitter edge—a perfect match for his poetic lyrics.

As for his guitar playing, both his fellow blues musicians and subsequent blues scholars and journalists agree that it almost single-handedly changed the soundscape of the blues forever. By playing a bass rhythm line with his thumb on the lower strings of his guitar, while simultaneously either using a slider or finger-picking the melody line higher up on the treble strings, Johnson was able to, in effect, sound like a small band. This tension between the bass and melody lines became the bedrock of modern urban blues in the post-World War II era. Robert Johnson's musical legacy can be heard in the blues bands of postwar urban blues giants such as Muddy Waters, Elmore James, Howlin' Wolf, Sonny Boy Williamson, and Jimmy Reed; he set the stage for their arrival. In addition, his music had a lasting impact on the legions of young white rock, folk, and eventually blues enthusiasts who emerged in the 1950s and 1960s.

MEMPHIS MINNIE

Memphis Minnie Douglas was the first woman schooled in a rural blues tradition to achieve national recognition and acclaim. Unlike the famous "classic blues" singers of the 1920s, such as Ma Rainey and Bessie Smith, who were groomed in black minstrelsy, Memphis Minnie's musical roots were in the Mississippi Delta. In addition, she was one of a select group of blues artists who played a pivotal role in the formation of a modern urban blues tradition. Not only was she the first well-known female to amplify her guitar and lead an urban blues band, but she was also one of the first blues musicians living in Chicago to experiment with using an electric guitar in a small-ensemble setting. In effect, Memphis Minnie helped to pioneer the style that became the foundation of Chicago's urban blues sound. These impressive accomplishments made her one of the most popular and influential blues performers of her generation.

She was born Lizzie Douglas on June 3, 1896, in Algiers, Louisiana, but her family moved to Walls, Mississippi, when she was seven. Walls was located in the Delta on Route 61, about 15 miles south of Memphis. "Kid," as she was nicknamed by her parents for her spunk and preciousness, demonstrated an early aptitude for the local Delta blues. She learned to play the banjo at the age of ten, and one year later she was also playing the guitar. When she was 14, she began to sing and play for tips in the streets and parks in Memphis, and she soon became a regular member of the city's growing blues community.

Initially, she was known as Kid Douglas, but by the early 1920s, she was calling herself Memphis Minnie. During this period, she teamed up with guitarist Will Weldon, a native of Memphis. They played together as a duo in the clubs along Beale Street, lived together, and were eventually married. Weldon was an original member of Will Shade's famous Memphis Jug Band; he continued to work with the group after pairing up with Memphis Minnie, who also played with the group occasionally. The Memphis Jug Band was formed in 1924 and made a series of popular blues recordings later in the decade; it was the city's most important early urban blues ensemble. Many of Memphis' most talented blues musicians passed through the band in the 1920s and 1930s.

In 1928, Memphis Minnie divorced Will Weldon and soon thereafter teamed up with another blues guitarist, Joe McCoy; they were married a year later. McCoy had been involved in the blues scene in Jackson, Mississippi, along with his brother Charlie McCoy, the Chatmon brothers, Tommy Johnson, and Ishaman Bracey, before relocating in Memphis. Memphis Minnie and her new husband played regularly with Ned Davenport's Beale Street Jug Band in the local clubs and at Church Park, which catered exclusively to African Americans. They also played as a duo in a Beale Street barbershop that was a hangout for the city's blues musicians.

A Columbia talent scout heard them there in 1928 and signed them up for a recording session in New York City. They traveled to New York and together recorded a total of six songs for Columbia. Five were blues that McCoy sang and the sixth was Memphis Minnie Douglas' most famous song, "Bumble Bee Blues." Columbia Records, much to the firm's later regret, failed to release "Bumble Bee Blues," preferring to go with McCoy's songs. The husband-and-wife team were both

Memphis Minnie was a pioneer in a musical medium dominated by men. She wrote her own lyrics and accompanied her singing with masterful guitar playing. Her early experimentation with the electric guitar greatly influenced a later generation of blues artists including Chuck Berry and Muddy Waters.

polished guitarists, and they played together brilliantly, but Joe McCoy's blues were fairly commonplace, and his vocal style left much to be desired. Hence their Columbia recordings did poorly in the race-record market, and they were not asked to do any further sessions by the company.

Columbia's loss was Vocalion's gain. The talent scout for this Chicago-based race-record operation was Mayo Williams. During a field recording trip to Memphis in the fall of 1929, he signed up McCoy and Douglas and recorded them on the spot. Unlike his predecessors, however, Williams focused on Memphis Minnie's material and showcased her as a vocalist. Vocalion's first release by the duo, "Bumble Bee Blues," went on to become one of the best-selling blues records of 1930.

It was a sexual blues that highlighted the duet's dexterous guitar playing and Memphis Minnie's strong vocal style. She sang the blues with great authority, economy, and toughness. Her voice was very direct, almost blunt; she slightly slurred her words, giving them a bluesy intonation. The instant success of "Bumble Bee Blues" catapulted her into the limelight as a female blues recording artist.

Mayo Williams returned to Memphis in the fall of 1930. This time around he recorded Memphis Minnie as his feature artist. She was backed up by not only Joe McCoy, but also the Memphis Jug Band, and she even got her younger sister Bessie included in the recording session. More important, Williams was able to lure her to Chicago with promises of additional recording sessions as well as club dates. She moved there with Joe McCoy that same year and remained based in Chicago for the rest of her career.

Once they were settled in Chicago's Southside black enclave, Douglas and McCoy began playing dates in the local clubs and continued to record for Vocalion as a duet. But by 1933, Memphis Minnie was branching out on her own. That year she recorded as a solo artist for Okeh Records in New York City, and she won first place in a Chicago blues contest, besting local favorite Big Bill Broonzy.

The next year, Minnie and Joe ended their partnership, and she began playing dates with Big Bill Broonzy. They became a fixture at the legendary "Blue Monday" jam sessions at Ruby Lee Gatewood's Tavern on the Southside. For the rest of the decade, Memphis Minnie worked off and on with Big Bill and a number of his close associates, including Robert Brown aka "Washboard Sam," Bumble Bee Slim, and Sonny Boy Williamson. During this period, she also recorded for the Decca and the RCA Victor Bluebird labels. In 1939, Memphis Minnie married her third blues musician husband, Earnest Lawlers aka "Little Son Joe"; they would remain together until his death two decades later.

By the early 1940s, Minnie was experimenting with an electric guitar in her band. The poet Langston Hughes saw her playing in a Southside club during this period and wrote that her guitar playing, "amplified to machine gun proportions," reminded him of "a musical version of electric welders plus a rolling mill." Along with Robert Nighthawk, Muddy Waters, and T-Bone Walker, she was an early pioneer of this crucial transition to amplification.

Memphis Minnie Douglas continued to record and play club dates in the Midwest and the South throughout the 1940s and into the 1950s. During the postwar era, she made records for the Okeh company again and then with Columbia Records after it bought out Okeh. In addition, she recorded for J.O.B., Checker, and Chess, all Chicago-based labels.

While she still performed as a headliner at her customary Southside blues venues, Memphis Minnie also played regularly in Detroit, and she opened a blues club in Indianapolis for a while with pianist St. Louis Jimmy Odem. In the mid-1950s, however, with Little Son Joe's health failing, the couple moved back to Memphis to be close to family and friends. Memphis Minnie performed rarely after returning to Memphis, and she participated in only one additional recording session.

Little Son Joe died in 1961; by that time, Memphis Minnie's own health was deteriorating. She lived in obscurity in a series of local nursing homes throughout the 1960s and died of a stroke at her sister Bessie's house in 1972. She was buried beside her third husband, Little Son Joe, in the New Hope Cemetery in Walls, Mississippi, her hometown.

In retrospect, Memphis Minnie Douglas was both a trailblazer in the formation of modern urban blues in the postwar era and a trailblazing woman in a musical genre dominated by men. She left a musical legacy of more than 100 recordings that spanned over three decades of blues development: from the acoustic Delta guitar duets and the Memphis jug bands of the 1920s to the electric Chicago blues groups of the 1950s. She was the composer of a number of popular urban blues standards, such as her first hit, "Bumble Bee Blues," as well as "Nothing but Rambling" and the classic "Me and My Chauffeur Blues." Her reputation among fellow musicians as a woman who could hold her own as a guitar player, vocalist, fighter, drinker, and lover was legendary. But because her gender made her an oddity in her chosen field, her pivotal role in helping to fashion the rural-to-urban blues continuum is often overlooked—or viewed as a fluke of nature.

As a female vocalist and songwriter, she bridged the gap between the classic blues divas of the 1920s, such as Ma Rainey and Bessie Smith, and the emerging urban blues stylists of the postwar era, such as Willie Mae "Big Mama" Thornton, Koko Taylor, and Etta James. And as a guitarist and bandleader, she was on the cutting edge of the crucial transition from an acoustic blues to an electric blues, which in effect revolutionized the music, paving the way for the rise of both rhythm and blues and rock-'n'-roll.

T-BONE WALKER

Texas guitarist Aaron "T-Bone" Walker was the first musician working in the blues tradition to experiment with an electric guitar. The technical and stylistic innovations he created as the result of his experimentation in turn revolutionized guitar playing throughout the entire spectrum of American popular music during the post-World War II era.

T-Bone Walker's role in this transformation sprang in part from his unique synthesis of two seemingly disparate black musical genres popular in Texas during his youth. They were the rural blues indigenous to the communities of black agricultural workers in East Texas, and the urban dance music—or jazz—played by local black swing bands in cities such as Dallas and Houston. Walker was a product of both traditions; he would later incorporate elements from each of them into his much-copied guitar style and into his flamboyant showmanship as a bandleader and vocalist. They became the bedrock on which he built his reputation as a major pioneer of postwar rhythm and blues and, by extension, the rock-'n'-roll of the 1950s and 1960s.

Aaron Thibeau Walker was born on March 28, 1910, in Linden, Texas, located in the northeast region of the state. His father, Rance Walker, was a lumber-mill worker; his mother, Movelia Jimerson, was a Cherokee Indian who played the guitar and sang the blues to him during his childhood. Toward the end of World War I, young Aaron and his mother moved to Oak Cliff, a black neighborhood in Dallas. By that time, he had acquired the nickname "T-Bone," which was derived from his middle name, Thibeau.

The Walker household soon became a center for blues musicians in Dallas. His mother's cousin, Marco Washington, played the upright bass with Coley Jones' Dallas String Band; band members often gathered at Walker's home for informal jam sessions on weekends. Marco Washington was also involved in getting T-Bone his first professional string instrument.

Two legendary Texas bluesmen, Blind Lemon Jefferson and Huddie Ledbetter, better known as Leadbelly, were regular visitors at the Walker house during this period. In addition, Aaron often guided Blind Lemon around the streets of Dallas, where they would play for spare change.

The musical versatility and inventiveness that characterized Walker's later career were nourished by the rich blend of blues and jazz sounds he heard in Dallas. The black community there was a musical melting pot, as well as a school for aspiring young musicians. T-Bone Walker not only became a skilled banjo and guitar player, he also learned how to play the violin, mandolin, ukulele, and piano.

After his apprenticeship with Blind Lemon Jefferson, he played with a string band in a regional medicine show, then with classic blues singer Ida Cox's vaudeville stage band, and with a local swing band formed by his high-school classmates—all before he reached his 20th birthday. This mixture of musical experiences put him in touch with

Aaron "T-Bone" Walker successfully blended his knowledge of the blues and jazz in his vocal styling and guitar playing. He first recorded his famous "T-Bone Blues" with Les Hite and His Orchestra in 1940; early in his career, he had toured with the group as a vocalist.

T-Bone Walker delivered electrifying performances filled with biting guitar solos and acrobatic stage antics. His experimentation with the electric guitar revolutionized guitar playing in all areas of American popular music.

a wide variety of African American musical styles.

Walker's indebtedness to the older rural blues school was documented in the first record he made for Columbia Records in 1929. The two titles, "Wichita Falls Blues" and "Trinity Blues," were solo efforts with T-Bone playing both banjo and guitar; they were clearly inspired by the style and material of Blind Lemon Jefferson. Yet the Lawson Brooks Band, in which Walker played guitar during this same period, was a 16-piece ensemble patterned after the popular "territory" bands of the day: Bennie Moten's group from Kansas City, Walter Page's Blue Devils from Oklahoma City, the Milt Larkin Band from Houston, and Terrence T. Holder and his Clouds of Joy and the Alphonzo Trent orchestra, both based in Dallas.

Because the Southwest remained relatively isolated from the influences of the commercial music industry, the territory bands were able to experiment more freely with fusing certain blues practices with jazz instrumentation. Most notably, blues vocal techniques were transferred to the musical instruments used in the brass and reed sections: in essence, the blues vocal became the blues instrumental.

The guitar started out as part of the rhythm section in the territory bands, but it soon emerged as a solo instrument, especially when electric amplification was added. Two Dallas musicians, Eddie Durham and Charlie Christian, were in the forefront of the transition to electric guitar in the jazz world, while T-Bone Walker is credited with being the first blues musician to amplify his guitar.

In the mid-1930s, Walker and his new wife, Vida Lee, moved to Los Angeles, California; they would remain based there for the rest of their lives. The "city of angels" still had a relatively prosperous black music scene, in spite of the ongoing Depression. Hence it was something of a haven for blues and jazz musicians, especially those from Texas and the Southwest. Sometime after Walker established himself as the bandleader at the Little Harlem Club, located in the Watts district on Central Avenue, he began to experiment with amplifying his guitar in jam sessions with fellow guitarist Eddie Durham and during the famous "Battle of the Blues" held at the club in conjunction with other blues headliners such as Wynonie Harris.

In 1939, Walker went on the road with the Les Hite Band; during this sojourn, he recorded "T-Bone's Blues" with the group on the Varsity label in New York City. Then back in Los Angeles in 1942, he recorded his first electric guitar solo on "Mean Old World" for the Capitol label. During the war years, Walker split his time between leading bands at the Little Harlem Club in Watts and the Rhumboogie Club in Chicago, Illinois. He also toured military bases in the United States to perform for the black troops stationed there.

T-Bone Walker reached the zenith of his career as a blues innovator during the postwar era. His recordings for the Black and White label in the late 1940s and the Imperial label in the 1950s established him as the premiere electric blues guitarist of his time. They included his two best-known compositions, "T-Bone Shuffle" and "Call It Stormy Monday," which became a rhythm-and-blues standard. Walker continued to tour and record throughout the 1960s, not only in the United States, but also in Europe, where he was especially popular in France. With the onset of the 1970s, however, his health began to fail him. Over the years, his penchant for drinking liquor and smoking cigarettes had resulted in stomach and then lung ailments, and he died in a Los Angeles hospital at the age of 64 on March 16, 1975.

During his 50-year career, Aaron "T-Bone" Walker made significant contributions to black popular music as a composer, vocalist, and bandleader. A few of his best-known songs, such as "Call It Stormy Monday," became American popular music standards; his relaxed vocal style was copied by numerous younger blues singers; and his early bands were forerunners of the popular post-World War II rhythm-and-blues groups. His spectacular advances in harmonic chording and his inventive use of single-string, jazz-influenced runs and arpeggios brought the electric guitar to the forefront of rhythm and blues, and then rock-'n'-roll. In the process, his groundbreaking guitar style influenced—either directly or indirectly—all of the premiere modern blues and rock guitarists who followed in his wake. They included everyone from B. B. King to Jimi Hendrix to Eric Clapton to Stevie Ray Vaughan.

Part Two

THE JAZZ CONTINUUM

The big-band jazz style known as "swing" so dominated American popular music during the 1930s and the war years that cultural historians often refer to the period as the "swing era." This new orchestral dance music was pioneered by an elite group of African American bandleaders and arrangers in the 1920s, the most influential being Fletcher Henderson, Don Redman, Luis Russell, Jimmie Lunceford, Erskine Tate, Earl Hines, Bennie Moten, and Duke Ellington. Unlike New Orleans jazz greats Buddy Bolden, Joe "King" Oliver, and Louis Armstrong, who came from working-class backgrounds, this select group of musicians came from the relatively small black bourgeoisie. And with the exception of Duke Ellington, who was self-taught like most of the New Orleans jazz musicians, all of these middle-class black bandleaders and arrangers had formal musical training—many of them at the university level. Indeed, they were living examples of W. E. B. Dubois' famous "talented tenth" thesis, which argued that a well-educated black elite was a prerequisite for the political and cultural advancement of the entire race.

Understandably, the classical training of these talented African Americans influenced them to initially develop a more European-oriented approach to jazz than was the case with their New Orleans counterparts. In particular, their musical education conditioned them to write big-band arrangements as if they were writing for a large choir: the melody was harmonized for a set number of voices, which were then assigned to the different instruments in the orchestra. In addition, the rhythm section was used to provide the melody with a standard number of beats to the measure. This was in stark contrast to the New Orleans ensemble style; it was more partial to African polyrhythms, which tended to separate the melody from the groundbeat, not vice versa. Moreover, the early New Orleans jazz style favored African-based polyphony over European harmony. And finally, it allowed much more individual and group improvisation than was the case in the early big-band jazz arrangements.

New York was the birthplace of the swing-band tradition. The city had been the hub of the music industry since its inception and employed more black musicians than any other urban center in the country. Not by accident, it was also the location of Harlem, which by the 1920s had become the largest and most dynamic black metropolis in the United States.

The decade was not only the era of the Jazz Age, but also of the Harlem Renaissance, perhaps the most influential African American artistic movement of the entire century. Jazz music and dance, floor shows, and nightclubs were all important components of Harlem's legendary nightlife milieu, which many saw as a vital expression of the ongoing cultural experimentation associated with the Harlem Renaissance. During the 1920s, most of the elite jazz nightclubs moved from downtown Manhattan to uptown Harlem, not only because

As did many other performers of the day, including Duke Ellington, Cab Calloway enjoyed his first real success at New York City's Cotton Club, where he is shown here with his orchestra and the Cotton Club Chorus in 1936. In the early 1930s, the club alternated between Calloway and Ellington for its top billing.

the enforcement of Prohibition was more lax there, but also because it was the fashionable place to be.

Many of these cabarets had nostalgic southern names such as the Cotton Club, Club Alabam, and the Kentucky Club; they were invariably

to black and white customers. All of these sites were important venues for the emerging jazz swing bands.

The African American dance-band tradition in New York City was pioneered by James Reese Europe and the famous Clef Club orchestras in the early 1900s. But Europe was killed by a band member in 1919, and his orchestra disbanded just as the Jazz Age was coming into vogue. The next major black dance band to emerge in the city was organized by Fletcher Henderson.

Henderson had studied classical piano most of his early life under the tutelage of his mother, Ozie Henderson, a prominent concert pianist and teacher. After majoring in math and chemistry at Atlanta University, he moved to Harlem in 1920 to seek work as a chemist. Finding no employment opportunities open to him in his chosen profession, he soon turned to the music industry. Henderson went to work for W. C. Handy and Harry Pace's Black Swan Record Company, the first African American-owned label in the business. He was employed as the music director and in-house pianist. In 1923, the studio band he put together accepted a full-time engagement at the Club Alabam, launching Henderson's career as an independent bandleader. A year later, the band moved on to the Roseland Ballroom, where it would establish itself as the premiere large jazz band of the era.

The size of Fletcher Henderson's orchestra varied from eight to twelve members, depending on who was available on a given night; this be-

Based in New York, the Fletcher Henderson orchestra received top billing at the Roseland Ballroom as one of the swing era's greatest dance bands. Henderson's greatest individual legacy to jazz was his work as an arranger.

bankrolled by white mobsters and featured black floor shows that included a large dance band. For the most part, they catered to a wealthy white clientele. On the other hand, there were also numerous smaller nightclubs, again mostly white controlled, that featured black jazz musicians and were open to both races. In addition, there were a growing number of dance halls in Harlem, such as the Roseland and Savoy ballrooms, that featured African American dance bands and were open came the standard size of most future swing bands. From the beginning, Henderson's group was blessed with first-rate jazz musicians, who immediately influenced the direction of the music they played. His early group featured saxophonist Coleman Hawkins, cornetist Joe Smith, trombonist Charlie Green, and clarinetist Don Redman, who also became the orchestra's major arranger.

Redman, a musical prodigy since his childhood, was a conservatory-trained musician with a budding interest in jazz. He was the first big-band arranger to divide the orchestra into separate reed and brass sections and then play them off against each other via the call-and-response patterns found in the blues and New Orleans-style jazz. For example, the reed section would play the melody while the brass section countered with short punctuation riffs. This innovation was at the center of the subsequent development of big-band jazz and swing.

Fletcher Henderson was only a competent jazz pianist, and he didn't become an accomplished big-band jazz arranger until late in his career. His major strength as a bandleader was his choice of band members. Over the ten-year period that he was able to hold his orchestra together, Henderson signed on the best jazz musicians in the country. They included trumpet players Louis Armstrong, Joe Smith, Tommy Ladiner, and Rex Stewart; sax players Coleman Hawkins, Benny Carter, Lester Young, Ben Webster, and Chu Berry; trombonists Claude Jones, Dicky Wells, Benny Morton, and

Jimmy Harrison; as well as clarinetists Don Redman and Buster Bailey.

Armstrong was an especially important addition to the band. When he joined Henderson's group in 1924, he was the most outstanding jazz soloist in the country; his ability to improvise and to "swing"—or to give a song that special sense of rhythm also referred to as "jazz"—was unsurpassed. With Don Redman, Louis Armstrong was able to transform Henderson's dance orchestra into a first-rate jazz band, the first of its kind in New York City.

After Redman left the group in 1927 to become musical director of the Detroit-based McKinley's Cotton Pickers, Henderson took over most of the arranging chores. He managed to keep his orchestra together until he went broke in the mid-1930s. Then in dire financial need, he sold his best big-band arrangements to Benny Goodman. These arrangements were instrumental in the Goodman band's subsequent rise to national prominence.

Next to Fletcher Henderson and Duke Ellington, the most notable African American bandleaders based on the East Coast during the swing era were Luis Russell, Jimmie Lunceford, and Chick Webb. Russell was born in Panama in 1902 and spent most of his youth there. He learned how to read music and play the piano from his father, who was both a professional musician and a teacher. In 1919, young Luis immigrated to New Orleans, where he worked as a pianist and arranger

In this vintage photograph signed by members of the band, Jimmie Lunceford and His Orchestra are shown arriving in Chicago for a private engagement. Lunceford's musical training included a degree in music from Fisk University in Nashville and study under Wilberforce J. Whiteman, the father of big-band bandleader Paul Whiteman.

with many of the city's most talented jazz musicians. Five years later, he moved on to Chicago to play with Joseph "King" Oliver's Creole Jazz Band.

Late in 1927, Russell left Oliver's band and moved to New York, where he formed his own band with a nucleus of musicians he had known in New Orleans; they were bass player Pops Foster and drummer Paul Barbarin, who anchored the rhythm section; clarinetist Albert Nicholas; and trumpeter Henry "Red" Allen. Additional band members included alto sax player Charlie Holmes and J. C. Higginbotham on trombone. The band's New Orleans musicians accounted for its emphasis on simple New Orleans ensemble-style arrangements and solo improvisation. Two of the group's best-known recordings from this period were the free-wheeling "Panama" and "Saratoga Shout," which was based on the traditional "When the Saints Go Marching In."

The heyday of the Russell band was in the late 1920s and early 1930s, when they developed

and recorded most of their original material. In 1935, Luis Russell became Louis Armstrong's musical director, and his band began to accompany the legendary trumpet player and entertainer on most of his dates. Russell remained with Armstrong for eight years, then he returned to New York and organized another big band before retiring from the music scene in 1948.

Where Luis Russell tended to recruit his band members from New Orleans musicians, most of the original sidemen with the popular Jimmie Lunceford orchestra came from Memphis, Tennessee. Lunceford himself was born in Fulton, Missouri, in 1902 and grew up in Denver, Colorado, where he gained his initial big-band experience playing alto sax in the local African American dance orchestra. After earning a degree in music from Fisk University in Nashville, Tennessee, Jimmie Lunceford moved on to Memphis. There he taught music at a black high school and organized his first big band, using both his high-school students and former Fisk classmates as sidemen.

The nucleus of the group was drummer Jimmy Crawford, pianist Edwin Wilcox, and saxophonist Willie Smith. Crawford was the architect of an assertive two-beat drumming pattern that became a trademark of the Lunceford band. Wilcox, like Lunceford, had majored in music at Fisk; he wrote and arranged many of the band's early numbers. Smith was the orchestra's leading soloist and the man most responsible for shaping the distinctive sound of the band's much-admired reed section. Although he was a multi-instrumentalist, Lunceford preferred to direct the group from out front with a baton; but on rare occasions, he would also solo on flute or play his alto sax with the reed section.

In the mid-1930s, Jimmie Lunceford's orchestra began to achieve national recognition. Subsequently, the group moved on to New York City for major engagements at the Lafayette Theater and the Cotton Club. Lunceford also added the talented trumpeter and arranger Sy Oliver to the band's lineup. Oliver's brilliant orchestral arrangements quickly became the nucleus of the band's repertoire; they were prominently featured in the group's recordings for the Decca label from 1934 to 1938. Among Oliver's best-known arrangements from these years were "Organ Grinder's Swing" and "'Taint What You Do."

At the peak of the band's popularity, Sy Oliver departed for a more lucrative position with Tommy Dorsey's orchestra. He was replaced by Gerald Wilson, yet another brilliant young trumpeter and arranger. Wilson's contributions to the band's repertoire in the early 1940s included "Yard Dog Mazurka" and the popular hit "I'm Gonna Move to the Outside of Town"; his orchestral arrangements would have a profound influence on Stan Kenton's progressive big-band jazz of the post–World War II era.

Toward the end of the war, Jimmie Lunceford lost some of his finest musicians, in particular longtime drummer Jimmy Crawford, alto sax great Willie Smith, and trombonist Charles "Trummy" Young, who was also the band's best vocalist. In spite of these losses and a decline in the group's popularity, Lunceford continued to lead his Harlem-based orchestra on national tours until his death in 1948.

The most popular big band among Harlem residents during the swing era was led by drummer Chick Webb, known as the "King of the Savoy." Webb was born in Baltimore, Maryland, in 1908; early in his life, he was plagued with a

Chick Webb (far left), Ella Fitzgerald, and Louis Jordan (alto saxophone, far right) are pictured here performing around 1938 at Harlem's Savoy Ballroom, where the Chick Webb orchestra was an institution for a decade beginning in 1927.

tubercular spine, which left him hunchbacked and unusually short. He began to play the drums as a youth in local Baltimore dance bands, then moved up to New York for a shot at the big time while still in his teens. By 1927, Webb was leading his own orchestra, the Harlem Stompers, at the famous Savoy Ballroom; he would remain a fixture there over the next decade. The key sidemen in Chick Webb's initial band were trombonist Jimmy Harrison, the group's best soloist, and saxophonist Edgar Sampson, a fine arranger. Like Don Redman with Fletcher Henderson's big band and Sy Oliver with Jimmie Lunceford's orchestra, Sampson wrote most of the material for Chick Webb's Harlem Stompers. His most famous jazz compositions included "Don't Be That Way" and "Stomping at the Savoy."

From all accounts, Chick Webb's big band was at its best during the freewheeling "cutting contests" that were held periodically at the Savoy Ballroom. In these musical competitions with the other major swing bands of the day, Webb and his sidemen were invariably declared the winners. Of course, they had the home-crowd advantage. But the group was also legendary for being able to stretch out an arrangement to 20 minutes or a half hour, with the momentum of the music, driven forward relentlessly by Webb's furious drumming, building and build-

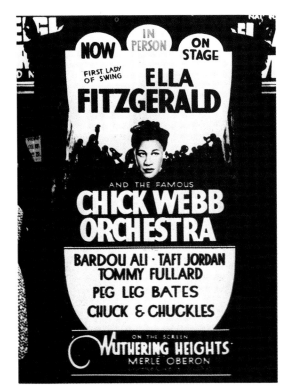

The Chick Webb orchestra achieved its greatest fame after Webb signed Ella Fitzgerald as lead vocalist in 1935. Fitzgerald's successful singing held the band together for several years after the death of their leader in 1939.

ing to a final crescendo. Unfortunately, none of these extended big-band jam sessions were ever recorded.

In 1935, Chick Webb added a young female vocalist named Ella Fitzgerald to the band's lineup. She was born in Norfolk, Virginia, and grew up in a New York orphanage; when she was 16, Webb found her singing in an amateur night at the Apollo Theater. Almost overnight, the popularity of the bandleader's discovery came to rival his own, leading to even greater success for the band. It signed a lucrative long-term record contract with the Decca label and toured nationally, setting attendance records all over the country. Yet as Ella Fitzgerald's star was rising, Chick Webb's was fading. His always delicate health took a turn for the worse in 1938, and he died a year later. Webb's band stayed together for a few years after his death under the nominal leadership of Ella Fitzgerald, but it wasn't the same without his dynamic drumming, and the group eventually disbanded during the war years.

Of all the African American big bands located on the East Coast during the swing era, Duke Ellington's orchestra had the most profound influence on the development of jazz and American popular music as a whole. Ellington began his musical career in his hometown, Washington, D.C., where he was the pianist in a band that eventually became known as the Washingtonians. Most of the band members, including Ellington, moved on to New York City in the mid-1920s. Soon after their arrival, the band was spotted by an enterprising young white talent scout named Irving Mills, who signed Ellington and what was now his group to an exclusive management contract.

In exchange for 45 percent of the profits and royalties, Mills took over as the manager; it was an exorbitant price, but not particularly unusual in the early years of the race-record business. And to his credit, Mills opened certain music industry doors that were invariably closed to African Americans on their own. He negotiated a record deal with the Columbia label, and he got the band booked into the Cotton Club for what developed into a five-year run.

The Cotton Club showcased black entertainers for a rich white clientele, hence the pay was better than what the band members had been earning, even after Mills' hefty cut. More important, their extended engagement gave Ellington the time and space he needed to develop both his talent for composition and his band's unique tonal style of swing.

Irving Mills was paid well, to say the least, for his role in the Ellington success story, and he went on to become a major figure in the race-record business. He later managed Cab Calloway and the Mills Blue Rhythm Band, a black swing band he named after himself. As an equal partner in Ellington's musical career, Mills saw fit to add his name to the copyright on most of Ellington's compositions published during this period. This was a common practice among race-record entrepre-

neurs, which gave them half of the composer's royalties as well as all of the publisher's royalties.

In 1939, after more than a decade of artistic and financial success, Duke Ellington terminated his 14-year business relationship with Mills and Columbia Records. After the break, Ellington signed a new contract with RCA Victor's Bluebird label and infused his band with new talent. For the next three decades, he continued to compose an impressive range of music and to direct one of the

Duke Ellington is pictured here in a 1934 still from *Belle of the Nineties,* in which he and his orchestra accompanied Mae West, who also wrote and directed the film.

most highly acclaimed swing orchestras in the country, thus solidifying his reputation as both a jazz giant and a great American composer.

Long before the New Orleans jazz revolution reached New York City, it made its way up the Mississippi to river ports such as Memphis and St. Louis, then overland to cities such as Chicago and Detroit. This jazz migration out of New Orleans began in earnest with the closing down of the notorious Storyville red-light district by the U.S. Navy during World War I; it continued unabated well into the 1920s.

Memphis, the first major port up the river from New Orleans, was the home of a resilient blues and jazz tradition that dated back to the early 1900s, when W. C. Handy led one of the city's popular black dance bands. Jelly Roll Morton and other New Orleans-based musicians were well known in the tenderloin nightclubs, saloons, and theaters along Beale Street during this period. By the 1920s, Memphis was the breeding ground not only for a number of blues-oriented jug bands, but also for jazz-oriented dance bands such as the Jimmie Lunceford orchestra.

The next popular stop along the northern migration route was St. Louis, a city with a rich history of African American musical activity. The river port was a hotbed of ragtime piano professors in the late 1800s and had its own home-grown blues and jazz traditions by the early 1900s. In addition to the local music venues in the city's tenderloin, St. Louis was also the site where the famous Streckfus Line hired black dance bands to play on their fleet of riverboats that carried passengers up and down the Mississippi River. Consequently, most of the river port's best jazz ensembles played regularly for the Streckfus Line, including groups led by Fate Marable, Charlie Creath, and Dewey Jackson. Creath and Jackson were superior trumpet players who headed up various St. Louis jazz orchestras throughout the 1920s and 1930s. They both employed a mix of local and New Orleans sidemen. For example, one of Charlie Creath's best bands featured bass pioneer Pops Foster, drummer Zutty Singleton, and guitarist/vocalist Lonnie Johnson, all from New Orleans.

Pianist Fate Marable was something of a living musical institution with the Streckfus Line. He started playing on the riverboats in 1907; over the next three decades, he led and trained legions of black band members. Like Creath and Jackson, Marable employed many New Orleans musicians over the years; they included trumpeters Louis Armstrong and Red Allen, clarinetist Johnny Dodds, and drummer Baby Dodds. During the swing era, he was the first major bandleader to hire bass player Jimmy Blanton, who went on to become an innovative force in the Ellington orchestra.

In spite of steady employment and a large pool of talented musicians, St. Louis' large jazz orchestras never received much national recognition. They lacked exceptional arrangers like Don Redman and Sy Oliver, and none of them were able to sign with a major race-record label. As a result, their impact on the popular music of the swing era was minimal.

After New York City, Chicago was the next most important music industry center in the country. During the swing era, a number of major labels, such as Paramount, RCA Victor, and Decca, had race-record operations in the city. In addition, the nation's first African American disk jockey, Jack Cooper, had programs on several local radio stations. Cooper broadcast the popular black swing recordings of the day, while also promoting local jazz artists and activities.

Chicago's Southside African American metropolis was second only to Harlem in size and importance throughout this period. Hence there was plenty of work for experienced black musicians, especially in the bands that were regularly employed in the local theaters, ballrooms, and nightclubs. One of the first black jazz ensembles to have a lasting impact on Chicago's music scene was King Oliver's Creole Jazz Band, which in the early 1920s was based at Lincoln Gardens, a popular cabaret controlled by the city's notorious Prohibition-era mobsters. In addition to Oliver, the group also featured Louis Armstrong and Johnny Dodds as soloists. The influence of New Orleans jazz ensembles was further enhanced when Jelly Roll Morton's Red Hot Peppers stopped in Chicago for an extended engagement in the mid-1920s; it was during this period that Morton's band made its best series of recordings for the Victor label.

Chicago's most popular local swing bands

in the 1920s and 1930s were often led by Erskine Tate, a classically trained violinist and arranger from Memphis. Most of Tate's bands were part of the lavish stage shows presented in major Southside theaters such as the Vendome and the Michigan. At times, there were up to 18 musicians in these orchestras, rather than the eight to twelve members in a normal-size swing band. Over the years, virtually every leading jazz musician in Chicago worked for Tate; the list of luminaries included trumpeters Louis Armstrong, Freddy Keppard, and Jabbo Smith; pianists Earl "Fatha" Hines and Teddy Wilson; violinist Eddie South; and clarinetist Buster Bailey. Although he made periodic recordings throughout the swing era, Erskine Tate's orchestras never received much popular acclaim outside of the city.

Patrons line up at the Chicago Theater in 1943 to see the Erskine Hawkins Band and the Four Ink Spots, later known as the Ink Spots. Theaters like the Chicago featured a variety of entertainment, including name bands and films, before they were eclipsed by "movie theaters" in the late 1940s and early 1950s.

Early in his career, Earl "Fatha" Hines performed with Louis Armstrong; the revolutionary style of jazz piano playing with which Hines is credited mimics Armstrong's delivery of single trumpet notes. Hines was a major influence on Teddy Wilson, the first African American pianist to play with the Benny Goodman orchestra.

The Chicago swing band that enjoyed the most success nationally was organized and led by Earl "Fatha" Hines, the prodigious pianist and composer from Pittsburgh, Pennsylvania. Hines was raised in a musical family and classically trained on the piano from the age of nine. While still in his teens, he began playing in Pittsburgh jazz circles. He then moved to Chicago in the mid-1920s. After working with some of that city's best-known jazz bands, including a short stint with Erskine Tate's orchestra, Hines made a series of recordings with Louis Armstrong for the Okeh label. They included some of the most highly acclaimed Armstrong recordings of the decade and catapulted Earl Hines into the national limelight. His piano style was very advanced for the times: it fused East Coast stride-piano techniques with the piano blues of the southern barrelhouse circuit.

In 1926, Hines formed his first big band and began an extended engagement at the Grand Terrace ballroom. During the next two decades, he was based at the Grand Terrace when not touring nationally or recording in the studio. His records sold well enough for him to continue with the recording dates, and his piano style was emulated in swing bands throughout the country. Over the years, his band members spanned two generations of jazz musicians, from the swing generation of the 1920s and 1930s to the bebop generation of the postwar years.

Kansas City was the third major stronghold of swing-band activity in the country. After World War I, the city was taken over by the infamous Pendergast machine, an alliance of gangsters and Democratic party officials led by political boss Tom Pendergast. With the blessing of the city's police, judges, and elected leaders, the local crime syndicate ran a wide-open red-light district, which netted millions in gambling, drug and liquor sales, prostitution, and the operation of cabarets featuring black entertainers. At its zenith in the 1930s, the Kansas City tenderloin had a higher concentration of nightclubs and saloons presenting black music and floor shows than any comparable red-light district in the nation. The city soon became famous for both its distinctive swing-band style and its after-hours jam sessions. At these late-night cutting sessions, band members honed their improvising skills in freewheeling solo competitions and traded "licks"—or musical ideas—with each other.

Bennie Moten and George Lee, both Kansas City natives, organized the first successful big bands in the city. Lee, a ballad singer who also played saxophone, teamed up with his sister, vocalist and pianist Julia Lee. Their band, made up of a small horn section, piano, and drums, was modeled after the jazz ensembles that backed up the vaudeville blues singers on the TOBA circuit in the 1920s. Moten, on the other hand, was a student of ragtime; after starting his musical training playing baritone horn in a marching brass band, he studied piano with two of Scott Joplin's former pupils.

Bennie Moten formed his first band, a six-piece unit, in 1921. Their music was initially an instrumental style of ragtime, but by the time the band made their first series of recordings for the Okeh label in the mid-1920s, they were mostly backing up vaudeville blues vocalists Ada Brown and Mary Bradford. As a result, close to three-quarters of the songs they recorded at these sessions were blues numbers.

Bennie Moten's band continued to add new sidemen and to explore a fusion of blues and jazz elements in their material well into the swing era. The orchestra benefited greatly from a steady influx of Texas jazz musicians who had worked in black dance bands in cities such as Dallas, Houston, and San Antonio; the best known were saxophonists Ben Webster and Eddie Barefield, trumpeter Joe Keys, and trombonist Dan Minor. But even more important was the demise of the legendary Blue Devils swing band, and Moten's ability to recruit most of its exceptional sidemen into his orchestra.

Based in Oklahoma City, the Blue Devils were considered to be one of the premiere bands in the Southwest in the late 1920s. But with the onset of the Depression, their bookings dried up, as was the case with other swing bands in the region, and the group finally disbanded in the early 1930s. Many of the ex-Blue Devils then moved on to Kansas City and joined Bennie Moten's band; they included saxophonists Buster Smith and Lester Young, trumpeter Oran "Hot Lips" Page, trombonist Jap Allen, pianist William "Count" Basie, bass player Walter Page, blues singer Jimmy Rushing, and trombonist/arranger Eddie Durham, who also was experimenting with an electric guitar in the band. After these additions, Moten's band made a

Bennie Moten's band played aggressive dance music with roots in New Orleans-style jazz and ragtime. One of their most popular songs was "Moten Stomp." Recorded by Victor in 1927, it won the band many a cutting contest in its heyday.

series of recordings for the Victor label that were comparable to the masterpieces of the swing era's best big bands. But in 1935, tragedy struck; Bennie Moten died after undergoing a minor operation. Count Basie eventually took over the leadership of the group. Moten was only 39 years old at the time of his death and at the height of his career as a bandleader.

The swing-band style that evolved in Kansas City and the southwestern region of the United States differed significantly from the style developed by the big bands based on the East Coast. The premiere eastern orchestras, like those led by Henderson and Ellington, relied more on elaborate melodies, complex arrangements, and rich harmonies; while the southwestern ensembles, often called the "territory" bands by jazz histori-

ans, preferred to play simple "head" arrangements of blues or call-and-response riffs with few chord changes, which allowed for more extensive solo improvising. There were many first-rate territory bands based in Kansas City at the height of the swing era; they included Jesse Stone's Blues Serenaders, Andy Kirk and the Clouds of Joy, Harlan Leonard's Kansas City Rockets, and the Jay McShann orchestra. But undoubtedly, the premiere Kansas City swing band was the Count Basie orchestra.

After Bennie Moten's death, Basie revamped the band considerably. His first move was to rebuild the rhythm section; the new lineup was Walter Page on bass, Jo Jones on drums, Freddie Green on guitar, and the Count himself on piano. Basie's rhythm section soon became the envy of bandleaders all over the country; in the process, it set the standard for the next decade of big-band development. The four musicians perfected an even, four-beats-to-the-measure momentum that became the new rhythmic foundation for swing, replacing the older two-beat style. The other superior component of Basie's orchestra was the reed section, organized by alto sax veteran Buster Smith; it included baritone saxophonist Jack Washington and two rising tenor sax giants, Lester Young and Hershel Evans.

Count Basie's orchestra first achieved national prominence due in part to the efforts of John Hammond, a wealthy white jazz fan who dropped out of Yale to become an independent race-record

Count Basie is shown here at the piano with John Hammond (second from right) and two admirers. Hammond, the renowned jazz talent scout and agent who worked with Bessie Smith, Duke Ellington, and Billie Holiday among others, was instrumental in Basie's early success as a star bandleader.

producer and talent scout. Hammond had produced Bessie Smith's last recording session for the Columbia label out of his own pocket, and he was working part-time for the Brunswick label when, in 1936, he first heard the Basie band on short-wave radio. He was impressed enough to go to Kansas City to see the group in person at the Reno Club, the band's hometown base of operations. Afterwards, Hammond helped to arrange for a series of national bookings, a recording session, and eventually a major appearance at Carnegie Hall in New York City.

The late 1930s proved to be golden years for the Count Basie orchestra. The band was at its peak professionally, and it was enjoying a groundswell of national acclaim. When his contract with Decca expired in 1939, Basie signed on with Columbia Records. Then the advent of World War II caused a number of personnel changes in the Basie orchestra, including the loss of its best two soloists, Lester Young and Hershel Evans. However, the band survived the war years and continued to be one of the country's most esteemed swing bands well into the postwar era.

The swing era produced almost as many new vocal stars as it did celebrated instrumental soloists. Most of these singers were products of local or regional jazz traditions, which were usually reflected in their respective styles. For example, Louis Armstrong epitomized the New Orleans jazz vocal style, complete with scat lyrics, while Jimmy Rushing did the same for the blues vocal style that evolved along with the Kansas City swing bands. On the East Coast, the vocal talents of Ella Fitzgerald and Cab Calloway eventually came to overshadow the instrumentalists in the swing bands they sang with, then fronted, and finally led. In general, far more vocal numbers reached the pop charts than instrumental pieces.

In part, this was due to the three-minute time limit on 78 rpm disks, which made them better suited for simple Tin Pan Alley songs than for more complex instrumental jazz arrangements. The record-buying public had also come to favor lyrics with their melodies. Whatever the cause, it left the swing bands at a disadvantage; unless they had a popular vocalist, their record sales suffered. This situation led to the gradual ascendancy of the singer in swing-band music, often at the expense of the featured instrumentalists and the collectivity of the band as a whole. A classic example of this transition can be seen in the trajectory of Louis Armstrong's career during the swing era.

This early advertisement for Selmer trumpets featuring a young Louis Armstrong was probably taken in the late 1920s.

Louis Armstrong's career as a trumpet player began with bands led by Kid Ory, Joe "King" Oliver, and Fletcher Henderson. He started his recording career under his own name in 1925. In 1930, he started his own orchestra, with whom he is pictured here at New York's Radio City Music Hall in the early 1930s.

Armstrong initially gained national acclaim in the 1920s as a jazz instrumentalist, playing a cornet and then a trumpet in various bands; his melodic genius as a soloist made him the most influential black musician of his generation. During his early career, Armstrong also recorded a handful of vocal numbers. In particular, he introduced New Orleans scat singing to a national audience.

Scat vocalists used nonsense syllables in place of words to vocally simulate instrumental jazz solos; the practice dates back to the original New Orleans jazz bands of Buddy Bolden's era in the 1890s. But Louis Armstrong's most important contributions to popular black music in the 1920s were as a pioneering jazz instrumentalist, not a scat vocalist.

This situation was then almost totally reversed in the 1930s when Joe Glaser became Armstrong's manager. Glaser marketed Armstrong as a traditional African American entertainer rather than as a jazz innovator. One of the consequences of this commercial strategy was that Armstrong took on the persona of a stereotypical comic min-

strel for his stage act and his newly secured roles on network radio and in Hollywood films. In addition, he began to do more vocal numbers at his recording sessions, and his choice of songs gravitated toward the popular Tin Pan Alley standards of the day. His biggest hits of the 1930s and beyond were invariably vocal renditions of pop standards such as "After You've Gone," "When It's Sleepy Time down South," Cecil Mack's "S-h-i-n-e" and Fats Waller's "Ain't Misbehavin'."

It was due to these hit recordings, along with the network radio shows and the film appearances, that Louis Armstrong achieved national stardom in the entertainment industry during the swing era. This commercial trend then continued well into the postwar decades, when Armstrong was better known for his popular cover versions of songs such as "Hello Dolly" and "Mack the Knife" than for his prodigious talents as a jazz trumpeter.

In many ways, Thomas "Fats" Waller's career paralleled that of Louis Armstrong, whom he rivaled as the swing era's most popular black male vocalist. Both began their careers as jazz instrumentalists, then evolved into pop vocalists; both utilized a comic minstrel demeanor in their stage acts and media appearances to achieve national fame. Moreover, both musicians hired veteran white managers to direct affairs at pivotal junctures in their respective careers.

Waller was raised in Harlem in the 1910s, where he was a pupil of stride-piano veteran James P. Johnson. Stride was an early East Coast jazz piano style more indebted to ragtime than the blues. In the 1920s, Fats Waller became one of Harlem's elite stride pianists; in addition, he began to write his own songs. By the end of the decade, he had already composed major hits such as "Squeeze Me"

and "Ain't Misbehavin'" and was at his peak as both a jazz pianist and a pioneering jazz organist.

Then at the onset of the swing era, Waller hired Phil Ponce as his manager; radio bookings, cameo film roles, and lucrative recording contracts soon followed. In the late 1930s, when Fats Waller reached the height of his commercial popularity, his public image was that of a happy-go-lucky comedian who sang the pop standards of the day—some of which happened to be his own compositions.

During this period, he teamed up with lyricist Andy Razaf; together, they wrote some of their most enduring songs, including "Honeysuckle

Fats Waller (seated center with hat and cane) is pictured here with the Les Hite orchestra and the Creole Dancing Chorus Revue in Los Angeles in the 1930s. Hite was a successful West Coast bandleader throughout the 1930s and into the 1940s, when he retired to become a booking agent.

Rose" and "Black and Blue." Unfortunately, Waller's comic image far overshadowed his genius for musical composition. In the early 1940s, his health began to fail him. Years of binging on alcohol and food finally took their toll, and he died in 1943 at the age of 39.

By far the most flamboyant of the swing-era vocalists was Cab Calloway. His outrageous onstage persona—that of a jive-talking hipster in a white satin tuxedo—took the music industry by storm in the 1930s, making him one of the most well-known black entertainers of the decade. Calloway was born in Baltimore, where he spent his youth before moving to New York City in the 1920s. There he launched his music career as a vocalist with various local swing bands. His first big break came in 1931 when he was booked into the Cotton Club for a long-term engagement by Irving Mills, who eventually became Calloway's manager. A major record contract with RCA Victor and national exposure on radio and in films followed later in the decade, catapulting the debonair Calloway into the limelight as a vocalist and bandleader. He became renowned for his extravagant showmanship and his scat vocals on numbers such as "Minnie the Moocher"—his signature piece—and "Knocking the Gong Around," with its veiled references to drug use.

Cab Calloway was also a fine judge of musicianship; over the years, he employed some of

Cab Calloway and His Orchestra were considered one of the most entertaining jazz show bands in the 1930s and 1940s. A creative, charismatic, and humorous man, Calloway frequently improvised on stage. His "hi-de-ho" scat singing earned him fame as a novelty singer and performer.

the best jazz sidemen in the country. At one time or another during the swing era, his orchestra included tenor sax titans Ben Webster, Eddie Barefield, and Chu Berry; trumpeters Doc Cheatham, Jonah Jones, and Dizzy Gillespie; trombonist Vic Dickenson; and a rhythm section anchored by drummer William "Cozy" Cole and bassist Milt Hinton.

Ella Fitzgerald and Billie Holiday were the two female vocalists based on the East Coast who achieved the greatest levels of success during the swing era. A Baltimore native like Cab Calloway, Holiday broke into the music industry in New York City, where her unique jazz vocal stylings caught the attention of producer John Hammond in the early 1930s. Hammond signed her to the Columbia label, and, over the next decade, he supervised the recording of her most memorable titles, such as "Lover Man" and "Strange Fruit," her theme song. Billie Holiday's understated and off-beat phrasing on these disks would influence jazz musicians and vocalists for years to come.

After a stint with Count Basie's band in 1937, she was hired as the featured singer with Artie Shaw's orchestra, becoming the first black female singer to work with an all-white swing band. In 1938, Holiday began a long-term engagement as the headliner at the Cafe Society, lower Manhattan's first integrated nightclub. The booking established her national reputation as a rising jazz star, but it also proved to be a fatal turning point in her promising career. During the engage-

ment, she became addicted to heroin; both her life and her career went into a tailspin from which she never recovered.

Ella Fitzgerald, on the other hand, continued to enjoy years of fame and good fortune even after the demise of the swing era that launched her career. While still with Chick Webb's band in the late 1930s, she had recorded

her first commercial hits, "A Tisket, A Tasket" and "Stomping at the Savoy." Later in her career, "the first lady of song" worked as a solo vocalist and relied almost exclusively on Tin Pan Alley standards by George and Ira Gershwin, Irving Berlin, Cole Porter, and Duke Ellington. Like Louis Armstrong, she became an international ambassador of American jazz in her travels around the world. Coincidentally, she was also well known for her versions of "Hello Dolly" and "Mack the Knife."

Chicago was the home base for both Joe Williams and Billy Eckstine, two prominent jazz vocalists who came of age during the swing era. In contrast to the comic minstrel demeanors of Armstrong and Waller, Williams and Eckstine developed suave and sophisticated stage personae that showcased their handsome physical features.

Williams grew up in Chicago, where he began his career as a vocalist with Jimmie Noone's

This photograph from the 1940s offers a rare backstage glimpse of Count Basie, Billie Holiday, and Billy Eckstine. During World War II, Eckstine formed a swing band which included Dizzy Gillespie, Miles Davis, Charlie Parker, Dexter Gordon, Art Blakey, and Sarah Vaughan.

Billy Eckstine was responsible for discovering Sarah Vaughan in the mid-1940s, when he signed her on as lead female vocalist for his swing band. They appear here on stage together in 1951. During the 1950s, Vaughn crossed over to the pop charts with such songs as "C'est la Vie" and "Broken Hearted Melody."

orchestra in the mid-1930s. Over the next decade, he was the featured singer in swing bands led by Les Hite, Coleman Hawkins, Lionel Hampton, and Andy Kirk. In the late 1940s, Joe Williams began a long-term association with Count Basie's orchestra, which gave him his first real national exposure. He recorded and toured with the Basie band regularly, becoming one of the major attractions in the postwar decades.

Billy Eckstine grew up in Pittsburgh but moved to Chicago in the mid-1930s, where he was the featured vocalist at the Club De Lisa. In the late 1930s, he joined Earl Hines' swing band; over the next four years, his recordings and appearances with the group won him his first national acclaim. During the war years, Eckstine formed his own swing band. It was made up of a virtual who's who among a new generation of black musicians that would collectively change the swing era's jazz soundscape by creating a new musical genre they called "bebop": trumpeters Dizzy Gillespie, Fats Navarro, Kenny Dorham, and Miles Davis; alto sax prodigy Charlie Parker and tenor saxophonists Dexter Gordon and Gene Ammons; drummer Art Blakey; and vocalist Sarah Vaughan. The band stayed together for only four years and recorded little of note. Nevertheless, it became something of a jazz legend, and Billy Eckstine remained active as a vocalist and bandleader for years to come.

Kansas City's romance with the blues was exemplified by the handful of vocalists there who came to the forefront during the swing era. Foremost among the Kansas City singers was Jimmy Rushing, a college-educated musician from Oklahoma City. The portly Rushing, known affectionately as "Mister Five by Five," began his career singing for the famous Blue Devils orchestra based in his hometown in the late 1920s. After the Blue Devils broke up, he signed on with Bennie Moten's Kansas City swing band in the early 1930s, and he remained with the group when Count Basie took over after Moten's death.

Jimmy Rushing was Basie's featured vocalist for almost two decades; during this period, he recorded some of his most enduring hits, including "Good Morning Blues" and "Goin' to Chicago."

His booming voice and his preference for blues numbers earned him the label "blues shouter"; in the process, he established a distinctive vocal style associated with the Kansas City jazz and blues fusion. Other vocalists who followed in his footsteps stylistically included Big Joe Turner, who would emerge as a popular rhythm and blues singer in the postwar years, and Jimmy Witherspoon, who launched his career with the Jay McShann swing band in the mid-1940s.

The big-band dance music associated with the swing era peaked in popularity during the late 1930s and the war years. Not coincidentally, a select group of white swing bands and vocalists rose to the top of the pop charts and the music industry during this same period. Benny Goodman, Jimmy and Tommy Dorsey, Bob Crosby, Harry James, Artie Shaw, Charlie Barnett, Woody Herman, and Glen Miller were the principal bandleaders; the major swing vocalists included Mildred Bailey, Helen Forrest, Frank Sinatra, and Bing Crosby.

The music created by all of these individuals, either directly or indirectly, was deeply indebted to the black swing-band musicians and traditions that preceded their ascendancy to stardom. For example, Benny Goodman used Fletcher Henderson's arrangements as the foundation of his big-band style. Moreover, he was the first major white bandleader to hire black sidemen; they were pianist Teddy Wilson, guitarist Charlie Christian, and vibraphonist Lionel Hampton, all of whom were employed by Goodman in the mid-1930s. The success of this racial experiment prompted many of the other leading white swing bands to follow suit: Tommy Dorsey hired arranger/trumpeter Sy Oliver away from Jimmie Lunceford's orchestra; Artie Shaw signed on Billie Holiday as well as trumpeters Hot Lips Page and Roy Eldridge; Woody Herman was strongly influenced by Duke Ellington and often used Ellington's sidemen on recording dates to augment his own band; and Charlie Barnett hired trumpeters Howard McGee and Peanuts Holland.

While the employment of black arrangers and musicians by white swing bands struck a blow against the color line in the rigidly segregated music industry, it also profited the bandleaders and their record companies. As had been the case in the Jazz Age and dating back as far as blackface minstrelsy, a pattern of black innovation and white popularization continued to dominate the music of the swing era. Initially created by black jazz orchestras in the 1920s, big-band swing was virtually taken over by an elite constellation of white swing bands and vocalists just as it was cresting as a popular musical genre.

BILLIE HOLIDAY

TOWN HALL · SATURDAY, FEBRUARY 16 · 5:30 p. m.

This original handbill advertises a Billie Holiday performance at New York City's Town Hall in 1944.

DUKE ELLINGTON

Undoubtedly, the most influential and highly acclaimed composer to emerge during the swing era was Edward Kennedy "Duke" Ellington. In retrospect, he is often characterized as a master painter who used his palette of big-band sounds to create some of jazz's most enduring masterpieces. His aversion to the standard eight- and twelve-bar pop song formats enabled Ellington to explore new song forms as had no other jazz composer before him.

In practice, most of Ellington's compositions were worked out improvisationally within the band. He started with a musical idea and, with the aid of his sidemen, shaped it into a simple song structure and then perhaps into a more extended jazz work. He was a genius at voicing together unusual combinations of instruments and at using dissonance as a counterpoint to harmony.

Over the years, he continued to mature as a composer and bandleader to a point where the two activities became inseparable. Today, Duke Ellington is remembered as one of this country's greatest 20th-century composers. His stature is such that he has elevated African American jazz to new heights of acclaim as an art form.

Edward Kennedy Ellington was born in Washington, D.C., on April 29, 1899. His father, James Edward, was a butler for a prominent white doctor, and his fashionable dress and penchant for elegant living made a lasting impression on his son. His mother, Daisy, was a homemaker who encouraged her son's artistic endeavors, especially on the piano, which she also played.

Ellington grew up in a comfortable, middle-class environment; by his teens, he was devoting most of his time and energy to music and painting. His schoolwork suffered, and he dropped out of high school before completing his senior year. By that time, he was completely immersed in the local black music scene, playing regularly with various combos in the clubs and for private dances.

In 1918, Ellington married his childhood sweetheart, Edna Thompson. Within a year, she gave birth to a son, Mercer. The couple separated nine years later, but they would never divorce, and Ellington provided for his wife and son for the rest of his life.

In the early 1920s, "Duke" Ellington, as he had come to be known in his hometown, became the pianist in a local dance band that eventually took the name the Washingtonians. The group included Sonny Greer on drums, Otto Hardwick on alto sax, Arthur Whetsol on trumpet, and the vaudeville veteran Elmer Snowden on banjo. All would move on to New York City in 1923. Their first venue was at the Hollywood Inn, located in midtown Manhattan's entertainment district; they stayed there for almost four years, during which time the name of the cabaret was changed to the Kentucky Club.

At first, the band played mostly commercial dance music, but the new sounds and styles of the Jazz Age were all around them, and they were fast learners—especially Ellington, who was now emerging as both a talented songwriter and the

Photo Bloom, Chicago

DUKE ELLINGTON
ET SON FAMEUX ORCHESTRE

(Page 57) Duke Ellington is featured on the cover of a French concert program dating from 1933. (Above) This poster announcing a Duke Ellington performance at a fund raiser in the early 1930s was designed by the noted African American cartoonist and graphic artist E. Simms Campbell.

central figure in the Washingtonians. A major personnel change in 1924 moved the band even closer to a swinging jazz style. Elmer Snowden and Arthur Whetsol left the group, Whetsol was replaced by James "Bubber" Miley, and clarinetist Sidney Bechet was added to the lineup.

Bechet was the finest reed player to come out of the New Orleans jazz mother lode during this period, and he was far ahead of his time as a lyrical solo improviser. He had a lasting influence on Johnny Hodges, a young alto sax player from Boston who joined the Ellington band a bit later. Bubber Miley had played the blues behind Mamie Smith and was a student of New Orleans trumpet great Joe "King" Oliver. In particular, he introduced Oliver's muting and growling horn techniques to the orchestra's brass section, which adopted them as a trademark.

Late in 1926, Duke Ellington signed a controversial management contract with Irving Mills, an entrepreneur who worked as a music publisher and booking agent. Ellington and Mills formed a corporation that gave each of them 45 percent of the profits and properties; the deal included Ellington's compositions. In return, Mills got the band its first major record deal with Columbia's race label and a long-term engagement at the Cotton Club, one of Harlem's most prestigious nightclubs showcasing black entertainers. Also, Mills owned half of everything Ellington wrote for his band, and Mills often listed himself as the co-writer on hit songs such as "Mood Indigo" and "The Mooch."

In any event, Ellington's swing band thrived under Mills' management; not only did it make a number of hit race records in the late 1920s and early 1930s, but Ellington and his group were also featured in a couple of Hollywood films, and they were heard on network radio.

Ellington was maturing as a jazz composer and arranger. He studied informally with Will Marion Cook and Will Vodery, two talented composers and arrangers from the famous Clef Club orchestras of the pre-World War I era; and he began to compose more extended jazz pieces for his orchestra, such as "Creole Rhapsody" and "Black and Tan Fantasy." When Ellington and his band first toured England in 1932, he was acclaimed as the United States' premiere jazz composer.

In 1939, Duke Ellington terminated his contract with Irving Mills and signed independently with RCA Victor's Bluebird label. By this time, Bechet and Miley were long gone; they had been replaced by clarinetist Barney Bigard and trumpeter Cootie Williams. Moreover, Ellington had also added Harry Carney on baritone sax and Puerto Rican Juan Tizol on trombone. After breaking with

Mills, he also signed on trumpeter Rex Stewart, tenor sax great Ben Webster, and Jimmy Blanton, a rising young bass virtuoso. In addition, Ellington brought the talented composer and arranger Billy Strayhorn into the group. Most jazz critics concur that this was his finest swing band; many of the musicians in the orchestra would remain with him throughout the rest of his career.

During the postwar era, Duke Ellington achieved his greatest success and recognition, both domestically and internationally. In the mid-1940s, he began a series of annual concerts at Carnegie Hall by premiering "Black, Brown and Beige," the first of many extended works written especially for the concert-hall performances. Notable events in the 1950s included the premiere of "Night Creature" at Carnegie Hall, with Ellington and band augmented by a symphony orchestra; a triumphant appearance at the 1956 Newport Jazz Festival; his own television special, "A Drum Is A Women" on CBS in 1957; and his first film score, "Anatomy of a Murder" in 1958.

During the next decade, Ellington continued to tour internationally, and he composed a series of "Sacred Concerts" for special performances in churches around the country. On his 70th birthday, Duke Ellington was the guest of honor at a White House reception hosted by President Richard Nixon, where he was awarded the Presidential Medal of Freedom. He continued to tour with his band up until his death from lung cancer in 1975.

Duke Ellington is pictured here with Chelsea Quealy on trumpet and Franz Jackson on saxophone in 1943 when the cream of jazz talent was invited to a jam session in New York sponsored by *Life* Magazine. Also in attendance were the Mary Lou Williams Trio and trumpet players Cootie Williams and Charlie Shavers.

COUNT BASIE

The Kansas City swing band led by William "Count" Basie in the late 1930s and early 1940s was one of the greatest musical ensembles in the history of jazz and by far the most dynamic big band to emerge during the culmination of the swing era. The Basie orchestra featured a number of gifted sidemen from the famous Southwest territory bands—including drummer Jo Jones, bassist Walter Page, guitarist Freddie Green, vocalist Jimmy Rushing, trombonist and arranger Eddie Durham, trumpeter Oran "Hot Lips" Page, alto saxophonist Buster Smith, and tenor saxophonists Lester Young and Hershel Evans. Ironically, the musician who was the glue that held the band together and who deserves a lion's share of the credit for introducing Kansas City jazz to a national audience hailed from Red Bank, New Jersey.

Initially he was known as Bill Basie in New York jazz circles and on the 1920s TOBA vaudeville circuit; the nickname "Count" was added by his Kansas City compatriots in the mid-1930s, probably to give him a royal title equal to that of Duke Ellington. His sudden rise to national prominence in the late 1930s was successfully sustained for many years thereafter, as the Count Basie orchestra became a fixture on the domestic and the international jazz scenes.

William Basie was born in 1904 in a small town near New York City. During his childhood, he showed great musical promise, mastering both the drums and piano before he was a teenager. By then, he was frequenting Harlem jazz clubs, where he found his first mentor, Thomas "Fats" Waller. After a year as Waller's understudy and then a stint with one of Elmer Snowden's jazz orchestras in the early 1920s, Basie tried the TOBA circuit for a while. He was the pianist for the Whitman Sisters and then the Gonzelle White Show, two vaudeville acts that toured nationally.

In 1927, Basie visited Kansas City with the Gonzelle White troupe, and he was so impressed with the local jazz scene that he remained behind when the show left town. Within a year, he was the pianist with Walter Page's Blue Devils, where he teamed up with a number of his future sidemen including saxophonist Buster Smith and trumpeter Hot Lips Page. In 1929, Bill Basie, trombonist Eddie Durham, and vocalist Jimmy Rushing left the Blue Devils to join Bennie Moten's orchestra, which at the time was Kansas City's leading swing band. Basie took over the piano chores, which enabled Moten to focus more on managing and fronting the band. When the Blue Devils broke up in 1931, Walter Page, Buster Smith, and Hot Lips Page were immediately added to Moten's lineup, which a year later would also include tenor saxophonist Lester Young. But just as Bennie Moten had assembled the best swing band in the Southwest and was on the verge of national recognition, he died during a routine tonsillectomy.

After Moten's death, the band decided to remain together, and Basie and Buster Smith became its coleaders. It was this group that record producer John Hammond heard during a live ra-

dio broadcast from the Reno Club in Kansas City in 1927. His proposal to get the band a major recording contract and set up a national tour was met with skepticism by Smith, who wished to stay in Kansas City. The rest of the group jumped at the opportunity, and Count Basie, as he was now called, became the sole leader of his own orchestra. While Hammond was trying to line up a record deal, Basie was approached by Decca talent scout Dave Kapp. Desperate for money for an upcoming tour, Basie agreed to a deal that paid the band $750 in advance for 24 recordings. Unfortunately, he did not read the contract's fine print, which awarded all of the artist's royalties to the label and committed

Count Basie and His Orchestra battled the Chick Webb orchestra in one of the classic cutting contests at the Savoy Ballroom in 1937.

the band to a three-year deal. The band never got royalties from their biggest hits of the decade, such as "Swinging the Blues," "Jumping at the Woodside," and "One O'Clock Jump"—the group's theme song, and John Hammond stated later that the Decca contract was the "most expensive blunder in Basie's history."

In spite of this setback, Basie continued to

adroitly steer his band into the national limelight. With help from Hammond and his music business associates, the Count Basie orchestra played a series of highly acclaimed dates in Chicago and New York in 1938. The next year, the band signed a major recording contract with Columbia Records, where the ever-present Hammond was working again as a producer. The two teamed up for a fine series of recordings during 1939 and 1940; among the best titles released from these dates were "Taxi War Dance" and "Drafting Blues."

Count Basie's Kansas City swing band was at the height of its creative powers when it burst upon the national jazz scene in the late 1930s. The rhythm section of Basie, drummer Jo Jones, bassist Walter Page, and guitarist Freddie Green sounded like a well-oiled engine. The saxophone section featured two of the most innovative soloists in the country, Lester Young and Hershel Evans, whose divergent styles gave the band its unique musical friction. Most of the arrangements for the orchestra were charted by Eddie Durham, who used much of the material developed under Bennie Moten's leadership. However, the core members of the group had played together for a long time, and most of them relied on "head" arrangements as well as solo improvisation.

In essence, the Count Basie orchestra during this period was still grounded in the Kansas City blues and riff traditions. The group was cohesive, it had great depth at the solo slots, and it had the most swinging rhythm section in the land.

Unfortunately, the band's personnel would change dramatically over the next decade, and the Kansas City influence would slowly fade. Nevertheless, the Basie orchestra would remain in the forefront of big-band jazz throughout the postwar era, in no small part because of the ingenuity and tenacity of its leader.

Basie was a gracious and easygoing individual, a portly musician more at home in front of a piano than in front of a prominent jazz band. Yet under his astute leadership, the band continued to prosper, even after its best Kansas City sidemen had long departed. No doubt the Decca royalties debacle made a lasting impression on Basie; his subsequent business decisions were less hasty, and they more than made up for the initial losses. After a decade with Columbia, he disbanded the orchestra for a while, then reorganized it in the early 1950s.

The revived Count Basie orchestra had an entirely new sound that was based on a mix of swing standards with the progressive jazz and bebop arrangements of Ernie Wilkins. While not as critically acclaimed as his Kansas City swing band, Basie's modernized jazz orchestra was much more successful financially, and it became a mainstay of big-band jazz for the next four decades. In the process, Count Basie evolved into one of the most revered and respected bandleaders in the history of black popular music; at the time of his death in 1989, he was a worldwide living jazz legend.

Count Basie is pictured here in the 1940s in a New York City recording studio with the singing team of the Nicholas Brothers. The photograph is by Austin Hansen, an African American who captured Harlem scenes and popular black performers of the 1940s, 1950s, and 1960s.

FATS WALLER

Thomas "Fats" Waller was the most beloved black musical figure of the swing era. His buoyant personality, humor, and repartee attracted legions of loyal fans—both black and white. From the mid-1930s up until his death in 1943, he was one of the most visible African American crossover entertainers in the country.

Not only was Waller a successful recording artist, he was also a popular radio and film star. His prominence as a black entertainer tended to overshadow his talents as a jazz musician and composer. Much like that of his contemporary, Louis Armstrong, Fats Waller's commercial success as a crossover act tended to undercut his development as a jazz artist. In spite of this contradiction, Waller's legacy to jazz in particular, and American popular music in general, was enormous. He was one of the most accomplished East Coast stride pianists of his generation, he pioneered the use of the organ in jazz circles, and he wrote some of the swing era's most memorable songs.

Thomas Waller was born in New York City on May 24, 1904. Both his parents were devout Christians, and his family attended Harlem's famous Abyssinian Baptist Church and often sang religious hymns at home, accompanied by his mother, Adeline, on her small harmonium. Young Thomas learned his first church songs on his mother's wheezy reed organ, but he was much more fascinated by the large pipe organ at the Abyssinian Baptist Church—which he also eventually mastered.

Waller began his musical career in his early teens, playing a pipe organ in Harlem's Lincoln movie theater. Already he was showing a preference for black popular music, which outraged his father. His mother, however, encouraged his new musical career. Then in 1920, Adeline died of diabetes. Thomas was only 15 at the time and closely attached to her. Her death removed one of the last moderating influences in Waller's life; from that point on, he was increasingly drawn to excessive eating, drinking, and high living.

In the wake of his mother's death, Waller married his childhood sweetheart, but the union, which produced two children, would be a short one. Soon after the honeymoon, he began to devote his life to his music and his merrymaking. The portly teen started to frequent the Harlem nightclubs that featured the best local piano professors. In the process, he acquired his nickname—"Fats"—and a new mentor, the renowned stride pianist and composer James P. Johnson. He not only taught Waller the basics of stride piano, but also music theory and composition.

In 1922, Waller made his first race record, backing up vaudeville blues diva Sarah Martin on "Ain't Nobody's Business If I Do." Throughout the rest of the decade, he was one of Harlem's most reputable stride-piano players, rivaling his teacher James P. Johnson and Willie "the Lion" Smith—both of whom he regularly engaged in cutting contests. Fats was also showing great promise as a composer, and his first race-record hit, "Squeeze

(Page 65) Fats Waller was a tremendous talent as a jazz composer and stride pianist.
(Above) Fats Waller made a brief trip to France in 1932. He appears here with a few American and French colleagues, including songster Spencer Williams, at Bricktop's nightclub in the Montmartre district of Paris, one of the city's most popular spots for jazz.

Me," was recorded and popularized by Louis Armstrong in 1928. A year later, Duke Ellington did the same for his composition "Black and Blue." During this period, Waller wrote a series of inventive piano compositions, which he recorded for the Victor label, as well as a number of show tunes used in black musicals.

Then in 1929, he wrote his two most famous songs, "Honeysuckle Rose" and "Ain't Misbehavin'"—the latter with lyricist Andy Razaf. But unfortunately, that same year he also sold his copyrights for these compositions and a number of others for $500 to pay off some of his mounting debts, which by now included delinquent alimony payments. The sale of these copyrights would cost him millions in future royalties.

Fats Waller achieved his greatest fame during the swing era. In 1932, he hired Phil Ponce, a white music industry veteran, as his manager. Under Ponce's guidance, Waller's floundering career

was revived, with radio providing the initial spark. Later that same year, Ponce negotiated a contract with WLW in Cincinnati, which launched the weekly "Fats Waller's Rhythm Club" on the station. WLW was the most powerful radio station in the Midwest, and Waller was soon well known throughout the region for his raspy vocals and his verbal horseplay on the air.

In 1934, after performing at George Gershwin's birthday party, Waller was approached by CBS president William Paley, who signed him to a network contract. For the next few years, Fats Waller hosted a biweekly variety show on CBS, as well as a Saturday night organ recital. Both programs were heard throughout the country and established his reputation as a pioneering crossover entertainer. During the 1930s, Ponce also negotiated two lucrative record contracts for Waller, initially with the Columbia label and then with RCA Victor. In 1935, Fats recorded his biggest commercial hit, "I'm Gonna Sit Right Down and Write Myself a Letter." Ironically, the song was not written by Waller—it was authored by a white Tin Pan Alley tunesmith.

Fats Waller's career as a popular entertainer peaked at the height of the swing era. In the late 1930s, he embarked on two successful European tours, performing for enthusiastic and overflowing crowds in a series of engagements in London and Paris. Back in the United States, he gave a solo recital at Carnegie Hall, where he premiered an ambitious and lengthy jazz composition entitled "London Suite." Unfortunately, the Carnegie Hall audience was more interested in hearing Waller sing and play his commercial hits than in his musical impressions of London, and the concert was panned by his fans and in the local press.

In the wake of his Carnegie Hall fiasco, however, Waller scored his greatest triumph as a popular entertainer. He made a cameo appearance in the 1943 Hollywood musical, "Stormy Weather," which also featured Bill "Bojangles" Robinson and Lena Horne. Two highlights of the film were Fats' vocal and piano rendition of his classic "Ain't Misbehavin'" and his witty repartee with the other actors.

By the early 1940s, his high living and over-indulgences were catching up with Waller. Since his teenage years, he had been both an alcoholic and a glutton, which accounted for his excessive weight and his diabetes. It was not unusual for him to eat ten hamburgers at one sitting, nor to

"FATS" WALLER

MAYO 1943   50 cts.   NUMERO 96

Fats Waller received considerable exposure outside of the United States during his brief but illustrious career. This Argentine jazz magazine, *Sincopa y Ritmo (Syncopation and Rhythm),* featured a jovial caricature of Waller on the cover of its May 1943 issue just months before his unexpected death.

drink two fifths of Old Grandad bourbon a day.

These abuses were compounded by a rigorous touring schedule and a penchant for late-night jam sessions. Eventually, Waller's health began to deteriorate, but he insisted on maintaining his breakneck pace. Then suddenly in late 1943, he died of bronchial pneumonia while on a cross-country train trip; he was only 39.

Fats Waller's funeral service was held at the Abyssinian Baptist Church in Harlem. Congressman Adam Clayton Powell, Jr., gave the farewell sermon and jazz organist Hazel Scott played a medley of Waller's best-known compositions on his favorite pipe organ. Thousands of mourners turned out to put Harlem's beloved son to rest.

Part Three

BEBOP AND THE BIRTH OF MODERN JAZZ

Even as swing reached a high-water mark in the late 1930s, there were signs of trouble on the horizon—in both the radio and the recording industries. In 1940, the American Society of Composers, Authors, and Publishers (ASCAP), the performance rights organization that collected royalty fees from the broadcasters for most of the leading swing bands, became embroiled in a dispute with the National Association of Broadcasters (NAB), the trade organization that represented the radio networks and their 600-plus affiliates. During contract negotiations, ASCAP demanded $9 million in performance royalty guarantees, almost doubling the rate of the previous agreement. The NAB not only refused to meet ASCAP's demand, but in retaliation, the networks and their affiliates dropped ASCAP's music from their airways, and the NAB set up a rival performance rights organization—Broadcast Music Incorporated (BMI).

Then in 1942, the American Federation of Musicians called a strike against the major recording companies, demanding higher recording fees and compensation for jukebox competition, which was taking jobs away from professional musicians. Swing-band recording sessions came to a virtual standstill for more than two years until the dispute was finally settled. In the interim, however, the swing era's leading vocalists, who were members of a different union, continued to make records. Needless to say, the recording hiatus adversely affected both the popularity and the payroll of the swing bands, as was the case with the radio boycott. For most of the war years, the two mass media outlets that had fueled the success of the swing bands in the 1930s were no longer accessible.

At the end of World War II, both the radio and the music industries embarked on a series of major structural changes, which continued to adversely affect the fortunes of the swing bands. In order to retool for the advent of television broadcasting, the two major radio networks—NBC and CBS—converted much of their national programming to a television format. However, their popular late-night live remote broadcasts of swing bands from different ballrooms around the country didn't translate into good visual programs, so they were eliminated.

Moreover, NBC and CBS left their local radio affiliates without their traditional programming fare. As a result, many turned to BMI as a cheap source of recorded music. Unlike ASCAP, BMI didn't charge radio stations the customary fee for playing their material; and while ASCAP continued to control swing music, as well as Broadway and Hollywood show tunes, BMI was building up a catalog of southern white country music and black urban blues—two genres of popular American music habitually ignored by ASCAP. The net result of these changes was that while airplay, and hence record sales, for country ballads and urban blues skyrocketed, the exact opposite was true for swing—it went into a tailspin.

In a photograph capturing his trademark full-cheeked playing style, Dizzy Gillespie is shown jamming at the Royal Roost in New York in 1948. Before he became widely recognized as one of the pioneers of bebop, Gillespie worked with many big bands of the swing era, including those led by Cab Calloway and Billy Eckstine.

To make matters worse, the economic underpinnings of the swing era were crumbling. Without the network radio connection, the ballroom dance circuit went into a sharp decline, depriving the swing bands of their major money-making venue. It became increasingly difficult to finance large dance orchestras, due to their size and escalating travel costs; smaller groups and solo artists were much more viable economically. The year 1947 proved to be the beginning of the end for the swing era; no fewer than a dozen major swing bands ceased to exist for financial reasons.

Among the best-known casualties were orchestras led by Benny Goodman, Woody Herman, Tommy Dorsey, Harry James, Billy Eckstine, and Benny Carter. As the list suggests, both black and white swing bands were breaking up because of the economic pressures of the postwar period. But the black big bands were also suffering from a defection in their ranks as scores of younger African American musicians joined the bebop revolution in jazz.

The bebop revolution dramatized a new generational shift taking place among African American musicians. The older black musicians had pioneered big-band swing in the 1920s and reaped some of its fruits in the 1930s, but their success was overshadowed by the emergence of the white swing bands. The younger generation of black musicians were initially schooled in the music of the 1930s swing bands, but they came of age just as the white swing musicians were cresting in popularity.

Partly in reaction to the white domination of swing and partly in reaction to the established commercial standards built into the music, the young lions of the bebop movement began to experiment with a new style of jazz improvisation. Within a few years, they not only created a uniquely original jazz genre, which they named "bebop," but along with their fans, they also founded a new black subculture.

Two interwoven jazz aesthetics, "hip" and "cool," were at the heart of the bebop subculture; they shaped its social habits of speech, dress, outlook, and lifestyle. To be hip was to be all-seeing and all-knowing, or wise beyond one's years; to be cool was to be mentally and emotionally unflappable, especially under duress.

These aesthetics were expressed through bebop's coded vernacular language, in which key words and phrases became double voiced. To the outside world, they maintained their conventional meaning and therefore made no sense; within the bebop subculture, however, they took on their intended meaning and made perfect sense. For example, the phrase "dig that chick" is unintelligible unless one knows what "dig" and "chick" signify to beboppers. Likewise, the standard bebop call-and-response greeting, "What's happening?" "Nothing but the rent!" is meaningless unless one is familiar with the ritual implicit in the greeting and its function within the subculture.

In addition to these habits of speech, the bebop community also developed a preference for certain illegal drugs and unusual dress. The drugs of choice were "reefer" or "Mary Jane" (marijuana) and "skag" or "horse" (heroin). As for fashion, beboppers liked to wear double-breasted "zoot" suits with suspenders, "shades" (dark sunglasses), and a wide assortment of "brims" (hats), from French berets to wide-brimmed felt fedoras to narrow-brimmed "porkpie" hats.

As could be expected, the bebop subculture and its music were purposely inaccessible to white people in general, and white swing musicians in particular. There were some exceptions, but generally speaking, the bebop revolution was a separatist cultural movement, calculated to put as much distance as possible between swing and bebop. In effect, it was the declaration of independence of a new generation of African American musicians.

The Harlem nightclub that became the launching pad for the bebop revolution was Minton's Playhouse—named after and owned by Henry Minton, a local black musician and entrepreneur. Late in 1940, Minton hired bandleader Teddy Hill to manage the club, and Hill set up a small house band that included drummer Kenny Clarke and trumpeter Dizzy Gillespie, two of his former band members. Hill's house band also featured pianist

Theolonious Monk, guitarist Charlie Christian, and eventually alto saxophonist Charlie Parker.

This core group of young black musicians became the early ringleaders of a musical revolution that would change the course of jazz. Returning to the small-ensemble format popular before the swing era, the group collectively worked out the basic harmonic and rhythmic changes that would become the foundation of bebop. Harmonically, musicians such as Parker, Gillespie, Christian, and Monk experimented with playing a greater range and combination of notes than was the case in the standard swing-band arrangements. Rhyth-

(Left to right) Pianist Thelonious Monk, trumpeters Howard McGhee and Roy Eldridge, and former swing-bandleader Teddy Hill pose in front of Minton's Playhouse in 1947. Beginning with Hill's management of the club in 1940, it was known for its experimental jam sessions improvised by bebop artists.

The essence of bebop, (left to right) Tommy Potter, Charlie Parker, Dizzy Gillespie, and John Coltrane are shown here performing at Birdland in 1951. During the 1950s, Birdland was a regular venue for all of the big names in bebop and modern jazz, including Miles Davis, Sarah Vaughan, and Dinah Washington.

mically, the band either accelerated the tempo up to and over 300 beats per minute, or they slowed the tempo down to under 100 beats per minute—especially on ballads. (Swing-band tempos were generally between 100 and 200 beats per minute—which were best suited for conventional dancing.)

All of the leading musicians in Minton's house band developed novel playing techniques subsequently emulated by aspiring young jazz musicians throughout the country. Charlie Parker was the group's diamond in the rough, and he soon emerged as the brightest luminary of the bebop rebellion. He was born and raised in Kansas City during the heyday of the Pendergast regime; at the age of 14, he dropped out of high school to become a swing musician. By that time, he had already taught himself how to play an alto saxo-

phone; he based his early style on those of Lester Young and Buster Smith, who became his mentor in the late 1930s.

In the early 1940s, Parker was a featured soloist with pianist Jay McShann's band, which was modeled after the more successful Count Basie orchestra. When McShann's group played Harlem's Savoy Ballroom in 1942, Parker became caught up in the local jazz scene developing around Minton's; the McShann band eventually moved on without Parker, who remained behind with his new bebop compatriots. During the next few years, he came into his own as a jazz soloist and innovator; his breakneck tempos and unique chord changes helped to trigger the bebop revolution. Moreover, Parker was one of the first jazz horn players to experiment with using all 12 keys in a standard scale, rather than just the 4 major keys favored by swing musicians.

As a result of these innovations, Charlie Parker became the most famous and influential bebop musician of the postwar era; his status was comparable to Louis Armstrong's in the 1920s. But during an extended stay in Los Angeles, his mental and physical health took a turn for the worse. He was committed to a state mental hospital at Camarillo in 1946 and remained there for almost a year. In 1947, Parker returned to New York to lead a group that included trumpeter Miles Davis and drummer Max Roach, but his health continued to deteriorate and his behavior became even more erratic. Parker had been addicted to alcohol and heroin since he was a teenager, and the consequences were finally catching up with him. After a long series of physical ailments and emotional breakdowns, he died at the age of 34.

Charlie Christian's short life was even more tragic. The legendary guitar player was just making his presence felt among the young lions of the bebop movement when, owing to personal negligence, he succumbed to tuberculosis in New York City at the age of 22. Christian was born in Dallas and grew up in Oklahoma City. His father was a blind guitarist who led a family string band, which Charlie joined at an early age. While still in his teens, he moved on to play with a series of territory swing bands based in Dallas, Oklahoma City, and Kansas City. It was in Dallas in the mid-1930s that he began to experiment with amplifying his guitar—along with Eddie Durham and T-Bone Walker.

By the late 1930s, Charlie Christian had developed a unique single-string electric guitar style: in effect, he used his guitar as if he was playing a horn solo. During this period, he was discovered by the ubiquitous John Hammond, who brought him to the attention of Benny Goodman. After an audition, Goodman hired Christian and brought him to New York, where his band was based. When he wasn't playing for Goodman, Charlie Christian could be found sitting in with the house band at Minton's Playhouse. Up until his death two years later, he was a major figure and an innovative force in the budding bebop rebellion.

Theolonious Monk, along with Bud Powell,

Drummer Max Roach was probably most influenced in developing his playing style by Kenny Clarke, whom he heard at Minton's Playhouse in the early 1940s. Roach was one of the bebop era's most active young drummers, working frequently with Charlie Parker, Dizzy Gillespie, Miles Davis, and Coleman Hawkins in the mid- to late 1940s.

worked out the basic bebop approach to the jazz piano during their tenure at Minton's Playhouse. Monk was born in Rocky Mount, North Carolina, but grew up in New York City, where he taught himself to play the piano. Initially, his major influences were Earl Hines and Art Tatum, the legendary blind Harlem pianist who was a forerunner of the bebop movement. It was Tatum who pioneered the use of accelerated tempos and a wider range of harmonies in jazz piano. Monk absorbed these lessons but rebelled against Tatum's precise technique. In its place, he opted for a minimalist approach to his instrument, relying on understatement and idiosyncrasy. In addition, he preferred very slow tempos, which was evident in many of his best compositions such as "Ruby My Dear" and "'Round about Midnight."

Thelonious Monk wrote many of the important innovative compositions of the modern jazz era, including "'Round about Midnight," "Off Minor," and "Straight No Chaser." For most of his career, he worked almost entirely on his own, or in small combos, performing regularly in New York City clubs.

Bud Powell became a regular at Minton's Playhouse after Monk befriended him and invited him to sit in with the house band. Powell was a New York native who grew up in a musical family and was classically trained on the piano. When he turned to jazz, he was initially influenced by Earl Hines and Art Tatum, as was Monk. But once Powell joined Minton's inner circle, he came under the spell of Charlie Parker. Powell worked out arrangements of Parker's solos with his right hand, while his left hand accented the bass line with dissonant chord progressions.

Within the bebop movement during the 1940s and 1950s, Powell's piano style became more the in-group standard than Monk's style because it was more accessible. But Powell's career crested in the mid-1940s, due to personal problems and heavy drinking. Over the next decade, he was in and out of mental institutions until his death in 1955 at the age of 31—yet another bebop musician who failed to reach his full potential.

Of all the key musical figures associated with the bebop revolution, John Birks "Dizzy" Gillespie achieved the greatest longevity and was ultimately the most prolific. He was nicknamed Dizzy because of his prankster antics on stage, as well as his velocity and range on the trumpet. Gillespie was born into a musical family from South Carolina, studied music on a scholarship at a private black school in North Carolina, and eventually migrated north, where he joined Teddy Hill's band in 1937. Two years later, he was a featured soloist in Cab Calloway's orchestra, which was based in New York City, but, due to his celebrated pranks and his evolving trumpet style, his stay was brief.

Like other bebop musicians of his generation, Dizzy Gillespie had started to experiment with new harmonies and different phrasing techniques. This led Calloway to accuse him of playing "Chinese music." Gillespie, however, was undaunted, especially since he had already joined the crew at Minton's Playhouse and would soon emerge as bebop's leading trumpeter. In 1945, Dizzy Gillespie and Charlie Parker collaborated on a series of recordings that included two numbers that would become bebop anthems—"Salt Peanuts" and "Now's the Time." These disks proved to be the most influential jazz records released since Louis Armstrong's sides with Earl "Fatha" Hines two decades earlier. Both series dramatically changed the soundscape of the music for years to come.

After working as the arranger and musical director of Billy Eckstine's orchestra, Gillespie formed his own big band in 1946; it survived for almost four years. During that period, the group was not only the premiere bebop orchestra of the postwar era, but it also pioneered the inclusion of Afro-Cuban rhythms and instruments within the band's format. Gillespie employed the legendary Cuban percussionist Chano Pozo, and along with a brilliant young composer named George Russell, they created the first Latin jazz classics, "Cubano Be" and "Cubano Bop." After the demise of his big

band, Dizzy Gillespie remained in the forefront of the bebop movement and firmly established himself as one of the leading jazz composers and trumpeters in the country. During his long career, he was able to supplant Louis Armstrong as the United States' ambassador of jazz around the world.

The bebop movement remained on the cutting edge of jazz well into the 1950s. The changes it brought to the music were so compre-

Dizzy Gillespie had his own big band on and off for about five years in the late 1940s. Featured with him are John Lewis on piano, Cecil Payne on baritone saxophone, and a young Miles Davis (second coronetist from left).

hensive that, in retrospect, bebop is generally viewed by jazz historians as modern jazz's first stage of development. By the 1950s, a new cadre of young bebop disciples had emerged nationally on the jazz scene. They included trumpeters Miles Davis, Fats Navarro, Kenny Dorham, and Clifford Brown; saxophonists John Coltrane, Dexter Gordon, Jackie McLean, Cannonball Adderly, and Sonny Rollins; drummers Max Roach and Art Blakey; and bassist Charles Mingus. Collectively, this group built on the musical changes pioneered by bebop's founding fathers.

Jazz was no longer a popular dance music under the thumb of the entertainment industry as had been the case during the height of the swing era. It was now more akin to an avant garde art form that required serious listening habits. But ultimately, bebop cost jazz much of its widespread popularity—among both the white and the black populace. The mass audience of the swing era gave way to a more selective audience in the postwar period. In effect, modern jazz not only abandoned the pop music mainstream, but it also severed its ties to the more functional dance music popular in the black community.

The musical vacuum created by the demise of swing was not filled by bebop; it was filled by urban blues, which by the late 1940s was being called "rhythm and blues." Nevertheless, bebop's hipster subculture would be emulated by future generations of cultural rebels—both black and white.

During the postwar period, a series of tech-nological advances set the stage for a radical restructuring of the record industry. The first of these advances was the introduction of magnetic tape, an invention stolen from the Nazis at the end of World War II. Prior to this innovation, most recordings were done in large and expensive studios located in major urban centers such as New York and Chicago, and invariably, these studios were owned by the large record companies. Magnetic tape decentralized recording technology, making it possible for anyone to record anywhere—all you needed was a tape recorder.

Then in 1948, Columbia's Dr. Peter Goldmark invented high fidelity. To capitalize on this innovation, Columbia introduced the 33 rpm, long-playing record (LP), which could hold up to 25 minutes of music on each side. This meant that an entire symphony could be recorded on one disk—or a lengthy jazz composition. RCA Victor, the other leading record industry giant, countered with the more compact 45 rpm record format, and the famous "battle of the speeds" was on.

These inventions not only made the 78 rpm disk obsolete, but they also accelerated the pace of decentralization within the record industry. More specifically, the 45 rpm disk was much cheaper to manufacture than the old 78 rpm model, while the LP had much more music on it. Consequently, two new commercial music markets opened up, and a growing number of small record companies were able to take advantage of them along with the major labels.

By 1950, there were more than 400 of these small independent record companies in business—most of which had been started after World War II. The most important were Atlantic in New York City; Savoy in Newark; Imperial, Modern, and Specialty in Los Angeles; Chess in Chicago; King in Cincinnati; and Peacock in Houston. All of these labels specialized in the regional rhythm and blues and, to a lesser extent, bebop—both of which were generally being ignored by the major record companies in the postwar era.

The LP proved to be an ideal format for the development of modern jazz in the 1950s. It allowed the more innovative musicians to experiment with recording extended compositions and live jam sessions, prospects that didn't exist with the three-minutes-per-side 78 rpm disk.

One of the younger jazz musicians who came to the forefront in the 1950s after his groundbreaking LP recordings was Miles Davis, the mercurial trumpeter from St. Louis. Davis grew up in a middle-class family—his father was a dentist. He became a jazz musician while still in high school, then moved to New York in 1945, ostensibly to study music at Juilliard. Once he got to New York, Davis immediately sought out Charlie Parker, with whom he worked off and on for the rest of the decade. At the time, Davis' playing style was a carbon copy of the high-powered,

upper-register bebop trumpet style pioneered by Dizzy Gillespie. But his range and technique were more limited than those of Gillespie, which proved to be a liability.

Then late in 1949, Miles Davis was involved in a series of recording dates on the West Coast that came to be known as the "birth of cool" sessions. The dates also included two prominent members of Claude Thornhill's orchestra, saxophonist Gerry Mulligan and arranger Gil Evans, as well as pianist John Lewis. In these sessions, Davis unveiled a trumpet style that broke sharply from the

As a teenager in East St. Louis, Illinois, Miles Davis received early exposure to Clark Terry, Charlie Parker, Billy Eckstine, and Dizzy Gillespie, all of whom he met when they performed locally. The Grammy Award-winning Davis was one of the originators of the "cool" jazz sound.

standard bebop licks he had been playing since he was a teenager. His new style was somewhat akin to the minimalist approach to jazz phrasing initially pioneered by Theolonious Monk: it was low key, sparse, muted, and nonchalant—the epitome of "cool" and a harbinger of things to come.

In the early 1950s, Miles Davis dropped out of the jazz scene to kick a heroin habit he had developed during his association with Charlie Parker. Davis managed to conquer his addiction and returned to jazz in the mid-1950s. He immediately formed his own group for a series of dates in New York and then for a series of recording sessions with two independent jazz labels—Blue Note and Prestige. Over the next few years, his band featured at one time or another three rising young saxophone titans—Sonny Rollins, Julian "Cannonball" Adderly, and John Coltrane.

In 1959, Davis signed a major contract with Columbia Records and then released the jazz LP of the decade—"Kind of Blue." In addition to Miles on trumpet, the album also featured John Coltrane on tenor sax, Cannonball Adderly on alto sax, and pianist Bill Evans, who also wrote some of the material and helped with the arrangements. This award-winning LP proved to be the definitive recording of cool jazz, and it established Davis as the country's premiere modern jazz trumpeter and bandleader. During the next decade, Miles Davis recorded two additional breakthrough albums: "Sketches of Spain," a fusion of jazz with modern Spanish classical music; and "Bitches Brew," a fusion of jazz with high-voltage electronic rock and soul. In the process, he became the most celebrated jazz musician of his generation.

The most accomplished and controversial modern jazz composer during the postwar era was Charles Mingus, who was also a leading jazz bassist during this period. Mingus was born and raised in the Watts section of Los Angeles. As a youth, he often attended the Holiness Church with his mother, and the raucous gospel music performed at these Sunday services, complete with a trombone chorus and congregational call-and-response singing, would later influence some of his most famous compositions.

Mingus began his musical studies while still in high school; he took courses in music theory and private lessons from Red Callander, a prominent swing bassist living in Los Angeles. By the early 1940s, Mingus was working in Louis Armstrong's orchestra, and later in the decade, he sold his first jazz compositions to bandleader Lionel Hampton. He also played in Kid Ory's New Orleans jazz band. Then in the early 1950s, Mingus

Among the most challenging and inventive of artists, Charles Mingus was an accomplished bass player and composer who stretched the medium of jazz to new heights. He was always improving on an earlier melody or arrangement, sometimes stopping midstream in concert to try something new.

turned his attention to bebop, participating in a number of recording and club dates with musicians such as Charlie Parker, Dizzy Gillespie, and Max Roach. Within a few years, he was one of the premiere bass players in the bebop movement.

Of all the jazz musicians who came of age in the postwar era, Charles Mingus had the broadest range of experience, having played bass in New Orleans, swing, and bebop ensembles. Moreover, he was knowledgeable about gospel music and urban blues, which he had followed since his youth. All of these influences came to bear on his jazz compositions, which matured dramatically in the 1950s.

Mingus, like his contemporary Charlie Parker, wanted his audience to feel the emotional fabric of his music. To accomplish this, he based his compositions on personal experiences, and he addressed some of the most controversial social issues of the day, which made him unique as a jazz composer. For example, "Goodbye Pork Pie Hat" was a tribute to sax great Lester Young, written soon after his death, while "Fables of Faubus" has as its subject Mingus' angry reaction to the Little Rock, Arkansas, school integration crisis in the mid-1950s. Needless to say, his musical portrait of the state's segregationist governor, Orville Faubus, is far from flattering. Other prominent protest pieces he wrote during the decade included the satirical "Oh Lord Don't Drop That Atomic Bomb on Me" and "Haitian Fight Song," which he said could have been called "Afro-American Fight Song."

Featuring (left to right) Percy Heath on bass, Connie Kay on drums, Milt Jackson on vibraphone, and John Lewis on piano, the Modern Jazz Quartet led the way in promoting jazz as a serious art form in the 1950s. This publicity photograph was taken by James J. Kriegsman, celebrated portrait photographer to the music industry.

In 1959, Mingus produced a groundbreaking LP entitled "Mingus Ah Um." For this album, he wrote a series of compositions that sought to recreate the emotional atmosphere and intensity of a Holiness Church service. The LP won kudos from jazz critics and fans alike, and it established Mingus as one of the most important jazz composers of his generation.

The group most responsible for promoting jazz as a serious musical art form in the 1950s was the Modern Jazz Quartet (MJQ), which featured John Lewis on piano, Milt Jackson on vibraphone, Percy Heath on bass, and Connie Kay on drums. The group grew out of Dizzy Gillespie's big band, which featured Jackson as a chief soloist and Lewis as the pianist and arranger. Heath and Kay were brought on board once Jackson and Lewis decided to form their own quartet.

Louis Armstrong and Billie Holiday are pictured here in the star-studded 1947 jazz musical, *New Orleans*. It was Billie Holiday's only feature film. Armstrong, who appeared in more than 20 movies, introduced the popular "Do You Know What It Means to Miss New Orleans?" in this United Artists release.

Milt Jackson and John Lewis were something of an odd couple in terms of influences and styles. Jackson was raised in Detroit's black ghetto and came up through the ranks to become the leading vibraphonist in the bebop movement; his forte was solo improvisation. Lewis, on the other hand, was from a middle-class background. He grew up in New Mexico, where he graduated from the state college with a degree in music. His musical influences included everything from European classical music to the modern big-band jazz that flourished on the West Coast for a brief period during the postwar era.

Where Jackson was a hard-line beboper who concerned himself with improvisational playing techniques, Lewis was an innovative jazz composer and arranger preoccupied with transforming the formal structure of conventional bebop compositions. To accomplish this, Lewis borrowed freely from European classical musical forms, applying their building-block approach to extended jazz compositions. Perhaps it was the friction between the MJQ's most forceful musical personalities that sparked its sudden rise to prominence in

the 1950s, as some jazz historians have suggested. More likely, though, it was the unique blend of Jackson's brilliant playing and Lewis' pioneering modern jazz compositions that catapulted the group into the national limelight. In the process, their formal attire on stage and Lewis' landmark compositions, such as their memorial recording of "Django" (a moving tribute to the great gypsy jazz guitarist from France), elevated the artistic status of modern jazz at home and abroad.

The jazz singers of the postwar era can be roughly grouped into two camps. One favored the more conventional styles developed by the swing-band vocalists and tended to rely on Tin Pan Alley tunesmiths for material. Among this group were women such as Ella Fitzgerald and Sarah Vaughan, as well as male crooners such as Nat King Cole, Johnny Mathis, Billy Eckstine, and Joe Williams. The other camp was more closely aligned to the bebop movement; it included vocalists such as Eddie Jefferson, Babs Gonzalez, King Pleasure, and Betty Carter.

Somewhere in between the two was Billie Holiday. In spite of her drug addiction and mounting personal problems, she remained the reigning queen of the jazz vocal up until her death in 1958. Her unique style drew on the blues, swing ballads, and bebop phrasing. In effect, she bridged the gaps between all three genres of black popular music. But her style of singing was not easily imitated, and Holiday attracted few proteges in her final years.

The vocalist who pioneered setting lyrics to bebop solo improvisations was Eddie Jefferson. A native of Pittsburgh, he began his musical career as a tap dancer and scat singer in the 1930s. Jefferson was an admirer of the saxophone solos of Coleman Hawkins and Lester Young, and late in the decade, he hit upon the idea of writing lyrics for them. His first successful venture was to put words to Hawkins' highly acclaimed version of "Body and Soul."

During the 1940s, Jefferson was attracted to the bebop movement and began writing lyrics for saxophone solos by Charlie Parker ("Parker's Mood," "Now's the Time") and James Moody ("I Got the Blues," "I'm in the Mood for Love"). By the early 1950s, when he moved to New York to join James Moody's group, Eddie Jefferson's rendition of "I'm in the Mood for Love" had already become the classic example of bebop vocalese. He remained with Moody for the rest of the decade and then moved on to work with Dizzy Gillespie. By that time, Jefferson was the most revered and copied bebop vocalist in the country.

The bebop vocal breakthrough pioneered by Eddie Jefferson inspired a number of fellow jazz singers to follow his lead. One such vocalist was Clarence Beeks, aka "King Pleasure," who teamed up with the cosmopolitan jazz chanteuse Blossom Dearie to first record and popularize Jefferson's version of "I'm in the Mood for Love" for Prestige Records. King Pleasure borrowed not only Eddie Jefferson's material, but also his vocal style—it was difficult to tell the two apart on their respective recordings.

The same could be said for Babs Gonzalez, a Newark, New Jersey, native who also worked with James Moody in the 1950s—initially as his manager and then later as a vocalist. Gonzalez's indebtedness to Jefferson is evident on the series of recordings he made in the 1950s, which included his popular Christmas satire, "Bebop Santa Claus."

Betty Carter was the first black female vocalist to forge a bebop singing style in the 1950s. She grew up in Flint, Michigan, and joined the Lionel Hampton orchestra as a vocalist in the late 1940s while still in her teens. Her first bebop recordings were made with King Pleasure in the early 1950s on the Prestige label in New York City. Later in the decade, she also collaborated with Ray Charles on a series of recordings for ABC Paramount. But for the most part, Carter worked as a solo vocalist with a small back-up band, and over the years, she became a mainstay on the jazz circuit, both domestically and internationally. The bebop vocal trend peaked in the late 1950s, a bit later than the bebop movement as a whole. However, bebop vocalese was now an intregal part of jazz's expanding vocabulary.

Best known as a master of the vibraharp, Lionel Hampton formed his own orchestra in 1940. He recorded prolifically and attracted a massive following during his 50-year career.

The jazz singers active in the postwar period who remained faithful to the more traditional swing vocal styles proved to have much more crossover potential than their bebop counterparts. Ella Fitzgerald, for example, not only had a string of popular commercial hits in the 1950s, she also won two coveted Grammy awards for her efforts on "But Not for Me" and "Mack the Knife." Likewise, Sarah Vaughan broke into pop charts during this period with Tin Pan Alley material such as "C'est la Vie" and "Broken Hearted Melody." The silky smooth vocals of Nat King Cole graced the pop charts from his 1942 debut hit "Straighten Up and Fly Right" up until "Unforgettable"—his final gold record, released in 1964. During his 22-year recording career with Capitol Records, the label sold an estimated 50 million Nat King Cole disks. In the process, Cole became a millionaire, and the Capitol label grew from its modest beginnings in the early 1940s into a major record label by the 1950s.

The only black male vocalist who even remotely rivaled Nat King Cole's crossover success during this period was Johnny Mathis, a San Francisco native who began his career as a jazz singer in the local clubs there. Mathis signed a contract with Columbia Records in the early 1950s. By the end of the decade, he had five singles that sold over a million copies, including "Chances Are" and "Misty"—his biggest hit.

By the end of the 1950s, jazz had reached a new plateau, both economically and culturally.

On the commercial front, the music was strong enough to launch the careers of the record industry's first successful black crossover vocalists— the most notable being Ella Fitzgerald and Nat King Cole. This was a significant departure from the segregated race-record market of the pre-World War II years. On the cultural front, jazz had become respectable in the wake of the bebop revolution, and it was beginning to attract attention as a serious art form.

One indication of this was the founding of the country's first jazz research center, the Institute for Jazz Studies at Rutgers University in 1953. Another was the founding of the country's first university-level jazz program, the School of Jazz at Lennox, Massachusetts, in 1957. Further indications included the initiation of numerous jazz concert series on college campuses and the initiation of yearly jazz festivals in Newport, Rhode Island (1954); Monterey, California (1958); and Chicago, Illinois (1959)—the last one sponsored by *Playboy* magazine.

Moreover, jazz's international appeal continued to accelerate. The United States government sponsored an increasing number of jazz tours to places such as Africa and the Middle East, while commercial markets and opportunities for jazz continued to expand in Europe and also in Japan in the postwar years. The music born in the saloons and bordellos of New Orleans was now being performed on the stages of metropolitan concert halls throughout the world.

The Nat King Cole Trio received acceptance from the mainstream American public through frequent performances on national radio shows. The group's appearance in films, such as *Killer Diller* (1948) and *Make Believe Ballroom* (1949), also contributed to their popularity and showcased their versatility as performers.

CHARLIE PARKER

Even before his death from a heart attack at the age of 34, the legend of Charlie Parker was larger than life. He was the archetypal bebop rebel: jazz genius, hipster, heroin addict, trickster, alcoholic, mental patient. After he died, the legend mushroomed, and it became more difficult to separate the man from the myth and the myth from the music.

Perhaps the best way to approach Parker is to begin with his music because clearly the music he played on his alto saxophone revolutionized jazz. His unique style triggered a paradigmatic shift from swing to bebop, which in turn ushered in the modern jazz era. Hence, first and foremost, Charlie Parker was a great musical innovator, undoubtedly the most important of his generation. His musical legacy is comparable to those of Louis Armstrong in the 1920s and Buddy Bolden in the 1890s. Like these other two black music pioneers, Parker developed an entirely new approach to the music.

Charles Parker, Jr., was born in Kansas City, Kansas, on August 29, 1920. His father, Charles, Sr., was a vaudeville song-and-dance man who abandoned the family when the boy was nine years old. Charles, Jr., was raised by his mother Addie Parker, who worked as a nurse; she encouraged his early musical endeavors and bought him his first alto saxophone.

At the age of 14, young Parker joined his high-school jazz band, the Deans of Swing. After his first year, Charlie dropped out of school, determined to become a jazz musician. He began to sit in at the famous after-hours Kansas City jam sessions, but he was unprepared for his initial reception. On more than one occasion, he was publicly humiliated by a veteran jazz musician who found his playing amateurish.

After a summer of "woodshedding," or studying on his own, in the Ozark Mountains and a series of practice sessions with Buster Smith, Charlie Parker returned to the Kansas City jazz scene with a vengeance. He not only won back his musical honor, but he also established himself as the hottest new horn player in town. In 1939, Parker joined the Jay McShann band, which included a number of other musicians formerly with the Deans of Swing, just before it left for an extended engagement in New York. He never lived in Kansas City again.

New York City was the center of the bebop movement in the 1940s, and soon after his arrival there, Charlie Parker became one of its brightest luminaries. By this time, he was being referred to as "Yardbird"—or simply "Bird" by his fellow musicians and his growing legions of fans. He quickly sought out and befriended other bebop musicians, particularly Dizzy Gillespie, and soon became a fixture at Minton's Playhouse and the other bebop jazz clubs along 52nd Street.

In 1945, Parker and Gillespie made a series of recordings for the Savoy label that proved to be bebop landmarks. They included the prophetic "Now's the Time," which saxophonist Paul Williams later turned into a rhythm-and-blues hit

To Gerri
Good luck
Charlie Parker

85

(Page 85) Charlie Parker poses for a publicity photograph. (Above) Pictured at a jam session sponsored by the music producer Norman Granz in the summer of 1952 are some of the giants of modern jazz: (left to right front) Barney Kessel, Charlie Shavers, Charlie Parker, Johnny Hodges; (back) Benny Carter, Flip Phillips, Ray Brown, J. C. Heard, Oscar Peterson, and Ben Webster.

called "The Hucklebuck," and "Koko," Parker's immortal revision of the swing standard "Cherokee." On "Koko," Parker's brilliant reorganization of the standard chord progressions at higher intervals revolutionized jazz praxis. Almost overnight, his new approach became a centerpiece of the bebop aesthetic and secured for its inventor a prominent place in jazz history.

Predictably, the rest of the country lagged behind New York when it came to welcoming the new bebop music. When Dizzy Gillespie and Charlie Parker appeared at Billy Berg's club in Los Angeles in 1946, they were panned by the city's jazz critics and shunned by the local jazz fans. After the engagement was aborted, Gillespie returned to New York, but Parker stayed on. No doubt Los Angeles' hostile bebop environment contributed to his subsequent emotional breakdown, which led to his commitment to the state mental hospital at Camarillo, just north of the city.

Within a year, a well-rested and drug-free Charlie Parker was released from Camarillo and returned to New York to resume his career. The next few years proved to be his most productive and his happiest. He formed his own small combo, which included Miles Davis on trumpet, Duke Jordon on piano, and Max Roach on drums, and recorded some of his most inspired solo improvisations with this group. In addition, he continued to explore new settings and textures for his music; in 1948, he made a series of recordings with Machito's Afro Cuban Jazz Orchestra, and a year later, he recorded an album of love ballads accompanied by a full contingent of symphony string instruments. During this period, he also married his fourth wife, dancer Chan Richardson; she bore him his first child, a daughter they named Pree. Charlie seemed to be settling down.

In the early 1950s, things started to go downhill for Parker once again. He was drinking heavily and back on heroin, and his playing was erratic at best. His health was deteriorating rapidly; the years of excessive eating, as well as excessive alcohol and drug use, had left him with a bad liver, a peptic stomach ulcer, and an enlarged heart. When his daughter died of pneumonia in 1953, his emotional problems also returned. He attempted suicide and was hospitalized for a while in the Bellevue mental ward. Then on March 9, 1955, Charlie Parker fell ill at the New York townhouse of a wealthy female jazz patron. He had a bad case of pneumonia, but he refused to go to the hospital, and a doctor was called in to treat him there. Two days later, Charlie Parker died of a heart attack while watching television. The jazz world had lost one of its greatest and most gifted musical innovators.

BILLIE HOLIDAY

Billie Holiday was born Eleanora Holiday on April 7, somewhere between the years of 1912 and 1915 in the city of Baltimore. She took the name Billie early on, supposedly because of her tomboy nature and her fondness for the screen actor Billie Dove. Her father, Clarence Holiday, was an aspiring trumpet player before his lungs were damaged by poison gas in World War I. Subsequently, he learned to play the guitar and abandoned family life when he went on tour with McKinney's Cotton Pickers, and later, the Fletcher Henderson orchestra. Her mother, Sadie Fagan, was half Irish and worked as a domestic.

When Billie Holiday was a young girl, her mother left her in the care of her grandparents and an older cousin while she sought better-paying work in New York City. It was in this household that young Billie apparently was subjected to frequent beatings and mental abuse. Left to fend for herself, she ran errands and cleaned for a local house of ill repute, where she heard her first recorded jazz, the music of Louis Armstrong and Bessie Smith. In the summer of 1927, Billie Holiday left Baltimore for New York City to join her mother. There she was rejected once again. Her mother found her a room in an apartment house run by the famed Harlem madam, Florence Williams, and Billie ended up turning tricks until she was arrested and had to spend a few months in the local jail on Welfare Island.

Billie Holiday got her first big break in the early 1930s, when she auditioned as a dancer in a Harlem nightclub. She bombed as a dancer, but she landed a singing job when the owner happened to hear her sing the blues after the audition. She moved on to sing at the Log Cabin in Harlem, where

she met John Hammond. He was so impressed with her singing that he introduced Billie to Joe Glaser, who signed her to a management contract that included a record deal with the Columbia label and prosperous bookings in local venues such as the Apollo Theater in Harlem. Beginning in 1936, John Hammond, her producer at Columbia Records, teamed her with Teddy Wilson to record "Did I Remember?" and "No Regrets."

For the next six years, Holiday worked with Wilson or in small bands organized by Wilson to record the songs for which she is best known—numbering in all more than 80 titles. Featured on this venerable collection of jazz recordings were many of the outstanding jazz musicians of the day, including trumpeters Buck Clayton and Roy Eldridge, as well as saxophone greats Lester Young and Johnny Hodges. During this period, she developed a close friendship with Lester Young, who was responsible for naming her "Lady Day."

Due again to the influence of John Hammond, Billie toured with the Count Basie orchestra between 1937 and 1938. After her stint with Basie, Holiday also toured with the Artie Shaw band, becoming one of the first black female jazz singers to perform regularly with a white swing band in the South. Needless to say, her experiences on the road with Shaw's swing band were difficult at best.

Billie Holiday was known to have dramatic mood swings, which she often allowed to affect her stage performances. Plagued by lack of self-confidence, deep depression, and loneliness, she embodied her songs with a great compassion that seemed to be derived from her tragic life. She sang the blues, loser love songs, and popular jazz ballads of the era with a sense of longing and desperation. So captivating was Holiday that she was said to bring patrons to the point of tears. Her singing was slow and hypnotizing, demonstrating a phraseology and cadence that was skillfully innovative.

However, her ever-changing personal life made for a stormy, hard-to-manage career. She continually put herself in self-defeating love relationships, choosing men who used her, stole from her, and got her hooked on drugs. In 1941, she married a drug addict, Jimmy Monroe, and was soon a user herself. Holiday's addiction to heroin lasted for the rest of her life and was undoubtedly the greatest contributing factor to her demise and eventual death. She was in and out of jail over the years for possession of illegal drugs, which hindered her performance and recording schedules. By the early 1950s, the effects of her debilitating vices began to destroy her health, appearance, and voice. She often found herself without any money, even after many successful years of lucrative earnings. Singing engagements decreased, and when she did perform, she was repeatedly too drunk to get through a song. Unfortunately, no one seemed able to help her. After a two-month hospital stay, Billie Holiday died in New York City on July 17, 1959.

The effects of drinking and a heavy drug habit apparent, Billie Holiday belts one out in a performance late in her career. Self-destructive behavior was a way of life for the incandescent singer whose emotional turmoil apparently sprang from childhood rejection and abuse.

Part Four

RHYTHM & BLUES: ROOTS AND BRANCHES

R hythm and blues emerged out of an amalgam of three diverse genres of African American popular music: swing-band jazz, urban blues, and urban gospel hymnody. Swing provided the danceable groundbeat, honking saxophone solos, and two distinct vocal styles, those of the pop-oriented crooners and the blues-oriented shouters. Urban blues' contributions included the electric guitar and bass, the boogie-woogie piano, the 12-bar blues song, and the folklore of the ghetto tenderloin. Gospel hymnody supplied the fervor and excitement of storefront church services, 8- and 16-bar gospel song formats, vocal techniques such as the use of falsetto and melisma, and close-harmony quartet singing—which inspired the rhythm quartets of the 1930s and the doo-wop groups of the 1950s.

Historically, the term "gospel" was first used by white Protestant evangelists in the 19th century to characterize their hymnody, which in turn was inspired by the plaintive hymns of Dr. Isaac Watts, the famous 18th-century English Methodist preacher and poet. Some of the most popular hymns attributed to Watts, such as "Amazing Grace," also ended up in the repertoire of folk spirituals created among African American slaves prior to emancipation.

After the Civil War, the spirituals continued to be the most popular religious music among rural black congregations in the South. Moreover, African American college groups such as the Fisk Jubilee Singers introduced the spirituals to receptive white audiences in the United States and Europe. In effect, they became (along with the famous black minstrel troupes of that period) the first African American performers to cross over into the white cultural mainstream.

During the Reconstruction Era, two distinct song forms associated with the spirituals came to the forefront; they were the up-tempo jubilees and the long-phrased melodies that came to be known as "sorrow songs." The jubilees evolved from ring shouts. These were ritualistic slave circle dances with roots extending back into West African culture, disguised as fervent prayer sessions. The sorrow songs, on the other hand, were more akin to the Watts hymns, but they also incorporated blues tonalities, as well as call-and-response song formats, into their makeup.

Around the turn of the century, African American sacred music went through a series of crucial innovations. During this period, the rise of black evangelism in the form of the Holiness, Sanctified, and Pentecostal religious sects led to the development of newer performing styles. In particular, these storefront churches began to experiment with using musical instruments, as well as rhythmic call-and-response singing and dancing, in their services.

About the same time, the first all-male vocal quartets began to emerge as a force in black sacred music. As early as 1902, the Dinwiddie Colored Quartet recorded a series of spirituals and minstrel songs in a close-harmony, a cappella style

Chuck Berry got his start in the music business in 1955 when blues great Muddy Waters put him in touch with Chess Records; the Chicago-based label quickly signed Berry to a recording contract. One of the original rock-'n'-rollers, Berry is pictured here performing his classic "duck walk."

for the Victor label. Within a matter of years, male quartets were the most popular vocal groups in black religious denominations throughout the country.

Also during this period, the Philadelphia Methodist minister Charles A. Tindley began to write and publish his most famous inspirational hymns, including "I'll Overcome Someday," which was later converted into the civil rights anthem, "We Shall Overcome Someday," and "Stand by Me," which was recycled as a rhythm-and-blues hit for Ben E. King in 1961. Tindley's pioneering "gospel songs," as they came to be called, fused the folk sentiments of spirituals with the melodic formats of Watts hymnody and paved the way for

the emergence of a new generation of gospel composers in the 1920s.

Gospel composers and performers were organized into a national movement in the late 1920s with the founding of the National Convention of Gospel Choirs and Choruses by Sallie Martin and Thomas Dorsey. Martin was a towering figure in the history of black gospel music for close to 50 years. As the leader of her own gospel ensembles, she groomed and trained a number of important female musicians and vocalists, including Dinah Washington. In addition, she was an energetic entrepreneur who founded the country's first black gospel publishing house in Chicago and, in collaboration with Thomas Dorsey, sponsored their annual gospel convention.

Dorsey was a former vaudeville blues pianist and composer known as Georgia Tom because he hailed from Atlanta. He worked as an accompanist with both Ma Rainey and Bessie Smith on the TOBA circuit and coauthored with guitarist Tampa Red the bawdy race-record hit, "Tight Like That." But after the death of his wife and baby daughter in childbirth in 1929, Dorsey returned to the church and the solace of sacred music. Soon thereafter, he composed his two gospel classics, "Precious Lord" and "Peace in the Valley," which established him as the most famous gospel composer of his generation.

The upsurge of male quartets in the black church continued unabated throughout the 1920s and 1930s. These groups usually sang both the tra-

The Golden Gates enjoyed considerable airplay on national radio during the 1930s and early 1940s, bringing their down-home gospel harmonizing to a mainstream American audience. In 1941, they were one of the few African American groups invited to perform at Franklin D. Roosevelt's inaugural gala.

ditional spirituals and the newer gospel compositions, but increasingly, a number of them also began to experiment with jazz. One of the earliest was the Norfolk Jazz Quartet, which was popular not only on the black vaudeville circuit in the 1920s but also among African American church attendees, who knew them as the Norfolk Jubilee Quartet. The group came out of the Tidewater region of Virginia; they first recorded in 1921 as part of the initial race-record boom and continued to make records for the next two decades.

The Tidewater proved to be a hotbed of male quartet activity. Along with the Norfolk Jubilee Quartet, the region also gave birth to the even more famous Golden Gate Jubilee Quartet in the early 1930s. Like their precursors, the Golden Gates also sang and recorded a mix of sacred and secular material. In addition to their commercial recordings, the group appeared regularly on network radio throughout the Depression.

Another hotbed of close-harmony quartet singing was located in and around the Birmingham and Bessemer region of Alabama, which by the 1930s had produced a number of prominent groups, including the Birmingham Jubilee Singers, the Kings of Harmony, and the Famous Blue Jay Singers. Unlike their Tidewater counterparts, all of these Alabama male quartets sang only religious material, and they did so in the traditional a cappella style.

By the 1930s, the black male vocal groups called "rhythm quartets" began to emerge as part

of the swing craze. The most successful were the Ink Spots and the Mills Brothers. The Ink Spots got their start as a swing vocal group on WLW in Cincinnati, the same radio station that showcased Fats Waller. In the mid-1930s, they moved on to New York City, where they did a radio show on WJZ and recorded for the Victor label. Their biggest commercial hit was "If I Didn't Care," a sweet-sounding ballad released in 1939.

The essence of the Mills Brothers' vocalese was their uncanny ability to imitate the various wind instruments used in swing bands; as a result, the Chicago *Defender* dubbed them the "human orchestra." The four brothers were raised in Ohio, where they began their career singing in local churches and on local radio stations. Their big breakthrough came in 1931, when they moved to New York City to headline a musical variety show on the CBS network. The national exposure made

Formed in 1934, the Ink Spots were matched only by the Mills Brothers as the super-stars of male vocal harmony groups. They remained popular through the 1960s and featured only a handful of different vocalists in their lineup throughout their 30-year career.

Sam Cooke (top left) is seen in this 1950s publicity photograph with the star gospel group, the Soul Stirrers. He joined the group as lead singer in 1949, when he was 18 years old. During his eight years with them, Cooke recorded such gospel favorites as "Touch the Hem of His Garment" and "Nearer to Thee."

them a household name within a few years and led to a lucrative recording contract. For the rest of the decade, the Mills Brothers were the most popular rhythm quartet in the country.

The postwar era is often referred to as the golden age of gospel music. It was a period that produced not only a new generation of gospel quartets, but also a royal line of great gospel divas. In addition, the grassroots gospel movement established its own concert circuit—known as the "gospel highway"—in urban centers throughout the country, and it attracted the attention of the new independent record labels specializing in African American popular music.

The new male gospel quartets broke with

the established close-harmony tradition in a number of ways. For instance, they invariably showcased a dynamic lead singer who then became the center of attention. This led to emphasizing the solo pyrotechnics of the lead vocalist at the expense of close-harmony singing. As a consequence, the other members of the quartet were relegated to the role of back-up singers. The postwar male gospel quartets also broke with tradition by adding musical instruments to their lineup, especially electric guitars and a rhythm section usually consisting of piano, bass, and drums. And finally, these quartets favored the newer gospel compositions over the more traditional religious material popularized in the prewar years.

During the 1940s and the 1950s, the two most popular and influential gospel quartets in the country were the Soul Stirrers and the Dixie Hummingbirds. The Soul Stirrers were founded in Tyler, Texas, in the late 1930s and featured R. H. Harris as lead singer. Harris pioneered many of the new gospel singing techniques including plangent falsetto phrasing, moaning melisma, and a delayed sense of timing that heightened the intensity of his vocals.

The Dixie Hummingbirds were centered around lead vocalist Ira Tucker, a South Carolina native influenced by the blues and Gullah folk music from his home state. Tucker used most of the same vocal techniques associated with R. H. Harris and rivaled his popularity nationally. Both of these gospel singers had an important impact on the singing styles of the postwar era's major male R & B vocalists. Harris, in particular, trained a young protege named Sam Cooke to replace him as lead singer in the Soul Stirrers. After his apprenticeship, Cooke went on to become the most popular gospel figure of his generation before embarking on a new career as a rhythm-and-blues star.

African American women have always played a major role in the evolution of black sacred music, especially as vocalists; hence it is not surprising that a number of them have come to the forefront of the gospel movement. Sallie Martin was gospel music's first great diva. Beginning in the late 1920s, she almost single-handedly organized the emerging gospel movement and served as its first female leader. She was also the director of one of the most influential gospel choruses in the country, and she was an inspirational gospel vocalist in her own right.

Martin's only female rival in the prewar era, in terms of popularity, was Sister Rosetta Tharpe, a blues-based gospel singer from rural Arkansas who accompanied herself on guitar. Tharpe was the first female gospel star to cross

over to the secular mainstream; in the late 1930s, she joined Lucky Millander's swing band as a featured vocalist and made a series of commercial recordings with his band shortly thereafter.

During the postwar period, the three most prominent gospel divas in the country were Roberta Martin, Clara Ward, and Mahalia Jackson. Both Martin and Ward were dynamic leaders, teachers, and vocalists in Chicago and Philadelphia respectively—the two main centers of gospel music at the time. New Orleans native Mahalia Jackson migrated north to Chicago in the 1930s to work as a vocalist with Thomas Dorsey. During the next decade, she emerged as the most famous female gospel singer of her generation, a status that was

The Clara Ward Singers were one of the premier female gospel harmony groups during the post-World War II period. They toured nationally in the Big Gospel Cavalcade of 1957 and were featured at the Newport Jazz Festival that same year. Clara Ward (top), was a major influence on Dinah Washington and Aretha Franklin.

cemented with a long-term recording contract with Columbia Records. All three of these women had a significant impact on the vocal styles of the major female R & B singers of the postwar era, including Dinah Washington, Ruth Brown, LaVerne Baker, and Aretha Franklin.

The rising popularity of gospel music in the postwar era was fueled by the gospel recordings released on independent record labels and the gospel shows heard on local radio stations, both of which targeted the black urban consumer. The independent record companies that were the most successful in marketing gospel records included Apollo and Savoy in New York City, Peacock and Songbird in Houston, and Specialty in Los Angeles. Apollo was the first label to record Mahalia Jackson, while Savoy's most popular gospel artist was the singing preacher James Cleveland. Songbird recorded the Soul Stirrers with H. R. Harris; Specialty recorded them with Sam Cooke. Peacock recorded the Mighty Clouds of Joy and the Five Blind Boys of Mississippi, featuring their famous lead vocalist Archie Brownlee.

Black-appeal radio stations such as WDIA in Memphis, WLAC in Nashville, WERD in Atlanta, and WOOK in Washington, D.C., all broadcast a wide variety of gospel as part of their weekly programming. These radio outlets introduced gospel music to a much broader cross section of the African American population, not to mention the curious white listeners who could also tune in to the shows. In retrospect, much of the enhanced visibility of gospel music during this golden age can be attributed to the relative abundance of gospel labels and radio programs throughout the country.

The secular roots of rhythm-and-blues grew out of the swing band and urban blues traditions. Beginning in the 1940s, the most notable swing contribution to R & B was the migration of saxophone players from the declining big bands into the up-and-coming rhythm-and-blues groups. Within a few years, slimmed-down horn sections and honking sax solos were centerpieces of the popular R & B "jump" bands, as these small combos were called. Similarly, swing vocal crooners

Louis Jordan headed the all-black cast of the musical comedy film short *Caldonia*, released in June 1945. A year later, a novelty number by the same name was Jordan's first hit to cross over from the race to the pop charts, in a cover version by white bandleader Woody Herman.

such as Nat King Cole and a youthful Ray Charles, as well as shouters such as Big Joe Turner, Bull Moose Jackson, and Big Maybelle, migrated into rhythm and blues, where they made major contributions to the ongoing development of the music.

The musician who best epitomized the connection between swing and rhythm and blues was one of the latter's founding fathers, Louis Jordan. He began his career as a swing musician. After a stint with Chick Webb's orchestra in the late 1930s as an alto saxophonist and jive-talking vocalist in the Cab Calloway vein, Jordan formed his own pioneering rhythm and blues combo, the Tympany Five. Its lineup included two horn players and a three-piece rhythm section, which along with Jordan made six band members in all. They played a mixture of urban blues ("Early in the Morning"), swing ("Choo Choo Ch' Boogie"), jive ("Reet Petite and Gone"), novelty tunes ("Ain't Nobody Here But Us Chickens"), and Jordan's own blend of swing and urban blues that he called "jump blues" ("Let the Good Times Roll").

The urban blues tradition, which originated in the 1920s and crested in the 1950s, infused rhythm and blues with a number of key ingredients. Foremost among them was the use of electric guitars, pioneered by musicians such as T-Bone Walker and Memphis Minnie Douglas in urban blues bands in the late 1930s and early 1940s. Subsequently, the electric guitar became a centerpiece not only in the postwar urban blues

bands but also in the new R & B jump combos which emerged in the 1940s.

The urban blues bands were also the first black groups to experiment with amplifying the bass to bring the groundbeat more to the forefront of the music they were making. This practice caught on in rhythm and blues, where the bass line was used to establish and maintain the basic dance beat—with help from the drums. Another rhythmic innovation that rhythm-and-blues groups borrowed from the urban blues tradition was the use of boogie-woogie riffs by their pianists and guitarists. Urban blues pianists such as Memphis Slim and guitarists such as John Lee Hooker first used these up-tempo riffs in small-band settings in the early 1940s; by the next decade, they were commonplace among R & B combos.

Muddy Waters and Howlin' Wolf were the two urban blues vocalists who had the greatest impact on R & B singers in the 1940s and 1950s.

John Lee Hooker was born in 1917 in Clarksdale, Mississippi, a hotbed of blues activity. He played with Robert Nighthawk and a host of other Memphis-based blues musicians prominent during the late 1930s and early 1940s. An important innovator of the urban blues, Hooker is known for his brash guitar and vocal sound.

Idolized for his silky smooth singing style and soulful piano playing, Charles Brown was most popular as a performer in the Los Angeles nightclub scene in the late 1940s and early 1950s. Brown, who was dubbed a "Sepia Sinatra" by the trade magazines, scored his biggest hit in 1952 with "Merry Christmas Baby."

market for rhythm and blues; hence it was also a trendsetter for the rest of the country. The city absorbed close to 200,000 African American migrants during the war years when well-paying jobs in the defense industries were plentiful; most of these migrants came from Texas. Watts expanded dramatically during this period, and the nightclubs along Central Avenue such as the Savoy Club, the Cobra Room, Cherryland, and Ivie's Chicken Shack were once again filled with people dancing and listening to live music. The swing bands, however, were going out of fashion and being replaced by the new R & B combos.

These groups usually included a guitar player, a pianist, a bass player, a drummer, a sax-dominated horn section, and a vocalist; they played an amalgam of Kansas City swing and electric Texas blues. The premiere West Coast R & B combos in the 1940s were led by T-Bone Walker, Roy Milton, Joe Liggins, Amos Milburn, and Johnny Otis. Walker and Milton, both natives of Texas, pioneered this small-band format in Los Angeles in the late 1930s; Liggins, Milburn, and Otis then brought it to fruition by the late 1940s.

The crooning ballad style popularized by Nat King Cole was another important component of West Coast rhythm and blues. Cole and his trio began their career in Los Angeles before moving

Waters' deep blues vocal style, complete with impassioned moaning and groaning, inspired numerous R & B singers; in addition, he was responsible for popularizing an electric version of Mississippi Delta slide guitar. Likewise, Howlin' Wolf's gravel-voiced ferocity, as well as his histrionic stage antics, were widely admired and often emulated in rhythm-and-blues circles—not to mention rock-'n'-roll.

A number of regional R & B styles began to coalesce in the 1940s; the major ones were invariably based in large cities such as Los Angeles, Chicago, New York, and New Orleans, where the music industry was thriving again in the wake of the Depression. Los Angeles was an early breakout on to national fame. Next to Cole, the other major "Sepia Sinatras," as they were called in the music trade magazines, who worked out of Los Angeles in the postwar era were Cecil Gant, Charles Brown, Ivory Joe Hunter, and Percy Mayfield. Gant scored the Los Angeles region's first big national R & B hit with his 1945 recording, "I Wonder," which sold more than a million copies. Like Brown and Hunter, he excelled not only as a vocalist, but also as a pianist and composer. Charles Brown's most enduring recording was "Merry Christmas Baby," which he wrote and recorded in 1952. The best songwriter in the group, however, was Percy Mayfield. His modern urban blues masterpieces, such as "Please Send Me Someone to Love" and "Danger Zone," were widely acclaimed and often recorded by his fellow musicians.

Rhythm and blues thrived in Los Angeles throughout the postwar years—in no small part because of the locally based independent record companies and radio stations that produced and promoted the music. The most important labels founded in the city during this period were Specialty, Aladdin, Modern, and Exclusive.

Except for the Exclusive originators, all of the founders of these black music companies were white males. Specialty was launched by Art Rupee in 1944; his roster of successful artists included Roy Milton, Percy Mayfield, and the Soul Stirrers featuring Sam Cooke, who later crossed over into rhythm and blues on the label. Aladdin was started by Leo and Ed Messner in 1946; they recorded the Nat King Cole Trio, Amos Milburn, Charles Brown, and Sam "Lightnin'" Hopkins, the folksy Texas blues bard from Houston. Modern was run by the four Bahari brothers: Saul, Jules, Lester, and Joe; they began their label in 1945 and recorded artists such as blues shouter Jimmy Witherspoon, R & B diva Etta James, and urban blues guitarists Lowell Fulsom, John Lee Hooker, Elmore James, and B. B. King. Exclusive was founded by Otis and Leon Rene, two college-educated African American brothers from New Orleans. Their label was based in Watts; in the 1940s, they recorded Joe Liggins and the Honey Drippers and Johnny Moore's Three Blazers, who proved to be their most successful artists.

The most popular Los Angeles radio outlets that played R & B disks in the 1940s were KRKD, with Dick "Huggie Boy" Hugg, and KPOP, with Hunter Hancock. Both men were among the first white disk jockeys in the country to play this music on the airways. During the next decade, Hugg and Hancock were eclipsed by Joe Adams and then the Magnificent Monteque, both of whom worked for KGFI. Monteque's broadcasts regularly attracted up to 75 percent of the Los Angeles basin's African American listeners. His famous invocation, "Burn Baby Burn," used to introduce the "hot" R&B hits he featured on his shows, later inadvertently became the battle cry of the 1965 Watts rebellion.

Chicago was the nation's most important bastion of urban blues in the postwar era. The city's raucous electric blues sound became an essential ingredient in the R & B mix on a national level. During the 1940s, 150,000 rural black migrants flooded into Chicago from the South; at least half of them came from the Mississippi Delta region. They crowded into the cramped Southside ghetto and then increasingly into the newer Westside ghetto. The Southside was already honeycombed with small neighborhood bars that featured live entertainment on weekends. It was in these clubs that the Delta musicians played their down-home style of blues for fellow migrant workers. The bars had names such as the White Elephant, the Boogie Woogie Inn, the Flame Club, the Plantation Club, Sylvio's, and Smitty's Corner. On the Westside, the open-air Maxwell Street Market became an important focal point of blues activity.

At the end of World War II, amplification of vocals and instruments became commonplace in Chicago's burgeoning blues scene. The city's blues sound grew louder, more intense, and more percussive. In addition to being featured in the local clubs or on Maxwell Street, it was also beginning to be recorded by local record companies and played on Chicago's airways.

The African American who brought the urban blues to Chicago's airways was Al Benson. He migrated to the Southside in the late 1930s from the Mississippi Delta. After working in local black vaudeville as a master of ceremonies, he started a radio show on WGES. Benson was immediately popular with his fellow southern black migrants because he was the first disk jockey in the city who spoke in their vernacular and played the music they loved. By 1948, he was doing shows on three different Chicago stations and training a cadre of apprentice deejays.

During the 1950s, Al Benson became a cultural magnate in Chicago's black community; along with his radio shows, he also did a weekly television program, produced R & B concerts at the Regal Theater, and launched his own record label. But it was as a disk jockey that Benson made his greatest contributions to his people. Almost single-handedly, he established a new format on radio in Chicago that opened the door to an influx of down-home blues deejays such as Sam Evans, Big Bill Hill, and Purvis Spann. Collectively, these African Americans kept Chicago's airways saturated with the blues throughout the 1950s.

The upsurge of urban blues shows on Chicago radio stations was economically linked to the rise of several local R & B labels during that same period. The two most influential were Vee Jay and Chess. Vee Jay was owned by a black couple, Vivian and James Bracken. The label specialized in Chicago-based doo-wop groups such as the Spaniels, the Dells, and the Impressions, as well as urban blues artists such as Jimmy Reed and John Lee Hooker.

Chess Records was founded in 1947 by Leonard and Phil Chess, two white brothers who operated a nightclub and a record store on the Southside. Their lineup was a virtual who's who of Chicago's urban blues giants: Muddy Waters,

Howlin' Wolf, Little Walter Jacobs, Sonny Boy Williamson II, and Willie Dixon. In addition, Chess recorded R & B vocal groups such as the Flamingos and rock-'n'-roll acts such as Chuck Berry and Bo Diddley.

Muddy Waters and Howlin' Wolf proved to be Chicago's greatest urban blues bandleaders and recording artists. Together, their bands schooled an entire generation of postwar Chicago blues musicians. Their music influenced the rise of rhythm and blues in the postwar era and the emergence of rock-'n'-roll in the 1950s; in the next decade, it also played a major role in the blues revival and the British rock invasion. During this same period, Little Walter and Sonny Boy Williamson II were Chicago's premiere harmonica players; they were instrumental in making the "Mississippi saxophone," as the mouth harp was called on the Southside, into a mainstay of the Chicago blues bands. The harmonica became a viable alternative to the saxophone in R & B combos nationwide.

Bassist Willie Dixon was not only the musical director in charge of virtually all of Chess' major urban blues recording sessions, he was also a prolific songwriter who authored most of Muddy Waters' and Howlin' Wolf's rhythm-and-blues hits. In retrospect, Dixon was more responsible for crafting the Chess label's definitive urban blues sound than any other musician on the roster. By the mid-1950s, Chess Records was one of the most successful independent labels in the entire country. When it was ultimately sold in the next decade, the asking price was in the millions.

Harlem continued to be the nation's largest black metropolis during most of the postwar era. As such, it supported a lively R & B scene in its local nightclubs and theaters. Moreover, the New York radio market had a number of popular black

At one time or another, all of these blues legends played together. They are: (left to right standing) vocalist and pianist Jimmy Rushing, guitarist T-Bone Walker, harmonica player Sonny Terry, guitarist Muddy Waters, bassist Willie Dixon, and (seated) guitarist Brownie McGhee.

music outlets. The pioneering R & B disk jockeys in the city during the 1940s were "Symphony" Sid Torin on WHOM and Al "Jazzbo" Collins on WNEW. By the end of the decade, a number of African American deejays could also be heard on New York's airways. They included Willie Bryant ("the Mayor of Harlem") and Ray Carroll on WHOM, Phil "Dr. Jive" Gordon and Nipsy Russell on WLIB, Tommy Smalls on WWRL, and Jack Walker ("the Pear Shaped Talker") on WOV. This relative abundance of R & B disk jockeys working in the New York market enhanced the visibility of the local rhythm-and-blues scene for fans and musicians alike. Their role in making the city into a major

Based in Washington, D.C., the Clovers were a popular vocal harmony group in the late 1940s and early 1950s. Like the Moonglows and the Midnighters, their vocal styling was more heavily influenced by the blues than by gospel. Their song "Love Potion No. 9" became a big hit as remade by the Coasters in 1971.

R & B center was comparable to those of the local black music venues and the independent record companies.

Within the New York City area, four key independent labels fostered the rise of rhythm and blues—Apollo, Savoy, National, and Atlantic. Apollo was launched in 1942 under the guidance of Ike and Bess Berman, a white couple who owned a Harlem record store. The label specialized in rhythm and blues and gospel; its best-known artists were Dinah Washington, the Five Royales, and Wynonie Harris in R & B; and Mahalia Jackson, Roberta Martin, and the Dixie Hummingbirds in gospel.

Savoy was owned and operated by Herman Lubinsky, a white record-store owner who started the label in Newark, New Jersey. Reputedly a devious businessman who seldom paid royalties to his artists, Lubinsky recorded jazz giant Charlie Parker, gospel singer James Cleveland, and R & B vocalists Big Maybelle, Nappy Brown, and Wilbert Harrison. National was founded by Al Green in 1945; he recorded blues shouter Big Joe Turner with boogie-woogie pianist Pete Johnson, Billy Eckstine's big band, and the Ravens, a pioneering R & B doo-wop group.

But it was Atlantic Records that had the greatest impact on rhythm and blues, both in New York and nationwide. The label was established by the Ertegun brothers, two sons of the Turkish ambassador to the United States. With considerable help from black arranger/songwriter Jesse

Stone, who first charted the label's up-tempo bass patterns; Jewish producer Jerry Wexler, who later became a partner in the company; and the white tunesmith duo Jerry Leiber and Mike Stroller, Atlantic surged to the forefront of rhythm and blues soon after its inception in 1949.

The company assembled the 1950s' most successful roster of black artists: LaVerne Baker, Ruth Brown, the Clovers, the Coasters, the Drifters, the Platters, Chuck Willis, Clyde McPhatter, Big Joe Turner, and Ray Charles. With these acts, the label produced 19 number-one records and 126 top-ten hits on the R & B charts during the decade. It was on Atlantic that Ray Charles recorded his secular revisions of select gospel standards, which in turn revolutionized rhythm-and-blues song structures and vocal techniques throughout the country, paving the way for the rise of "soul" music in the 1960s.

Atlantic talent scouts first heard Ray Charles singing and playing piano with a studio band in New Orleans, a city that became an important source of new musical talent after World War II. As the birthplace of jazz and the home of the Mardi Gras, New Orleans had developed a rich and diverse tradition in African American popular music in the prewar years, in spite of the fact that many of the city's leading black musicians migrated north. Unlike the other major urban centers of rhythm-and-blues activity, New Orleans did not have any homegrown R & B record companies. As a result, independent labels based in New York City and Los Angeles began to visit the city in the late 1940s to seek out new talent.

Atlantic not only discovered Ray Charles in New Orleans, it also recorded Roy Byrd aka "Professor Longhair," the founding father of New Orleans R & B piano. Longhair's unique mix of blues, boogie-woogie, and rumba patterns gave birth to the infectious New Orleans shuffle rhythms of the

An influential recording artist of the 1950s and 1960s, Ray Charles has led a dynamic rhythm-and-blues and pop career for more than 40 years.

103

1950s. In fact, there is a direct line from Fats Domino's R & B hits in the 1950s to Professor Longhair's whimsical rumba boogies in the 1940s and then all the way back to Jelly Roll Morton's "Spanish tinge" compositions in the 1920s.

Three of the top independent labels based in Los Angeles—Aladdin, Specialty, and Imperial—all regularly recorded New Orleans-based artists such as Guitar Slim, Roy Brown, Little Richard, and Fats Domino at Casimo Matussa's J & M Studios. These sessions featured the city's most gifted R & B musicians, including bandleader/arranger Dave Bartholomew, tenor sax virtuoso Lee Allen, and master drummer Earl Palmer. Bartholomew also directed the house band at the Dew Drop Inn, New Orleans' most famous nightclub during this period.

Most of the city's live R & B venues were based in black neighborhood taverns and bars. They were augmented by the musical activities of a large number of African American social clubs, which invariably featured music as part of their cultural endeavors. Many of these clubs also sponsored their own all-purpose bands. Hence New Orleans continued to be a fertile training ground for aspiring young black musicians in the postwar era.

Rhythm and blues broke into the New Orleans radio market in the late 1940s with the inauguration of the "Poppa Stoppa Show" on WJMR. "Poppa Stoppa" was the radio brainchild of Vernon Winslow, a black art professor at Dillard College.

He had initially approached WJMR with the concept of doing an R & B program featuring himself as the jive-talking Poppa Stoppa. But the station would only broadcast the show if Winslow, in return, would relinquish the host position and train a white deejay to take on the role of Poppa Stoppa. Winslow reluctantly agreed to the proposal, and the program became an instant success in the New Orleans region. Over the next few years, Winslow trained a cadre of white Poppa Stoppas for WJMR before finally getting the opportunity to host his own show as "Doctor Daddyo" on WEZZ. Throughout the 1950s, Doctor Daddyo was the top R & B deejay in the city, along with another African American radio jock, Larry McKinley on WBOX.

During the golden age of rhythm and blues in the postwar era, the persistence of racial segregation in the entertainment industry inadvertently lead to the development of a separate economic and cultural infrastructure for R & B, located for the most part in the major black urban centers scattered throughout the country. The main components of this infrastructure included the fabled "chitlin" circuit venues and the independent record companies, as well as the R & B deejays, the neighborhood mom-and-pop record shops, and the African American press.

The chitlin circuit referred to a string of theaters, dance halls, and large nightclubs in black urban ghettos that showcased the top R & B acts of the day. The premiere chitlin circuit venues were the black theaters such as the Apollo in Harlem;

the Regal in Chicago; the Howard in Washington, D.C.; the Lincoln in Watts; and the Daisy on Beale Street in Memphis. But there were also a number of prestigious chitlin circuit nightclubs such as the Dew Drop Inn in New Orleans and the Bronze Peacock in Houston.

Independent record labels such as Duke/Peacock in Houston, King/Federal in Cincinnati, and Sun in Memphis had an impact on rhythm and blues in the postwar period that was almost equal to that of Atlantic and Chess nationwide. Duke/Peacock was owned and operated by Don Robey, a streetwise African American businessman with suspected links to Houston's underworld. Robey was a reputed numbers boss who also ran

the city's most celebrated black nightclub, the Bronze Peacock. He began his career in the record business recording popular gospel quartets such as the Dixie Hummingbirds and the Five Blind Boys of Mississippi on the Peacock label. He then expanded his operation with the purchase of Duke Records to include the music of former Memphis blues artists Johnny Ace, Bobby Blue Bland, and Junior Parker, as well as Willie Mae "Big Mama" Thornton, the blues shouter who recorded the label's first R & B hit, "Hound Dog," in 1953.

The Duke/Peacock rhythm-and-blues sound featured swing-band arrangements with electric guitar solos and squalling brass riffs. Joe Scott was the arranger and producer most responsible for these musical trademarks. Other R & B artists on the labels included guitarist Clarence "Gatemouth" Brown, a youthful Little Richard Penniman, and Johnny Otis, who also worked as a West Coast talent scout for Robey.

King Records was founded in Cincinnati by Sid Nathan in 1945. Unlike most of the other independent record companies, the label specialized in both rhythm-and-blues and country-and-western material. Nathan, a white Cincinnati business-man, was smart enough to hire a black producer, Henry Glover, to supervise the R & B side of his operation. Glover

Clarence "Gatemouth" Brown learned the guitar from his father at a very young age and went on to become an important figure in the post-World War II blues scene. He is pictured here with deejay Dewey Phillips, who intro-duced many blues greats on his popular Memphis show.

was a college-educated swing musician who had played trumpet in the bands of Lucky Millander and Buddy Johnson. He had also worked as an arranger for Jimmie Lunceford. Under his direc-tion, the label signed saxophonists Earl Bostic and Bill Doggett, swing vocalist Bull Moose Jackson, and urban blues shouter Wynonie Harris.

In 1951, Ralph Bass, a veteran white inde-pendent record producer, joined Nathan in form-ing a second label, Federal. Bass then proceeded to immediately record Billy Ward and His Domi-nos, who gave the King/Federal operation its first big national rhythm-and-blues hit, "Sixty Minute

Man," that same year. The other major R & B acts that the labels signed up in the 1950s were Hank Ballard and the Midnighters, Little Willie John, and James Brown and His Fabulous Flames. All three artists scored big hits for King/Federal, but it was James Brown, "the hardest working man in show business," who by the end of the decade emerged as "Soul Brother # 1" among R & B fans.

Sam Phillips, the son of a white Alabama tenant farmer, founded Sun Records in his Mem-phis recording studio in 1952. At the time, Phillips had already produced B. B. King's first recordings as well as the initial sides by Howlin' Wolf's elec-trified Delta blues band. During its first few years of operation, the Sun label recorded many of the city's most promising blues artists, including har-monica players Junior Parker, Big Walter Horton, and James Cotton, and vocalist Little Milton Campbell. However, none of these musicians had a major R & B hit for Sun, and they all left the label after a short period of time. By the mid-1950s, Phillips was scouting around for new recording prospects. In particular, he was looking for "a white man who had the Negro sound." He found one in Elvis Presley and then another in Jerry Lee Lewis. In the process, his fledgling label helped to ignite the rock-'n'-roll revolution in American popular music.

Memphis was also an important radio out-let for rhythm and blues in the postwar period. The first local station to play R & B was WHBQ. As was the pattern elsewhere, it initially employed white disk jockeys such as "Jitterbug" Johnny Poorhall and Dewey Phillips to host its rhythm-and-blues shows. A second Memphis radio outlet, WDIA, began to switch to a "black appeal" format in 1949. Under the guidance of Nat D. Williams, the city's first African American deejay, the station skyrocketed into the number-one spot in the local radio market. Among its most popular black disk jockeys were B. B. King, Rufus Thomas, Maurice "Hot Rod" Hulbert, and Martha Jean "the Queen" Steinberg. King and Thomas went on to successful careers as performers in the music industry, while Hulbert and Steinberg moved on to become the leading R & B disk jockeys in Baltimore and Detroit respectively.

The first African American-owned radio station in the country was WERD in Atlanta, which was purchased by businessman J. B. Blayton in 1949. Blayton hired Jack "the Rapper" Gibson as the station's first black program director; Gibson was a veteran of Chicago radio, where he had worked as an actor and a disk jockey. In addition to hosting WERD's most popular R & B show, he also staffed the station with African American personnel including deejays. Within a matter of months, WERD had cultivated one of the largest local black listening audiences in the nation.

The radio station that probably had the most African American listeners in the entire country was WLAC, a Nashville-based 100,000-watt, clear-channel AM outlet heard throughout the Deep South. The station shifted to a nighttime R & B format in the early 1950s; over the next two decades, its three best-known disk jockeys—Gene Noble, Hoss Allen, and John Richburg—developed a massive listening audience. Even though these deejays were white, a large number of their listeners were African Americans because the station was their only source of rhythm and blues.

This widespread pattern in which white disk jockeys attracted a mixed audience by playing rhythm and blues on the airways was something of a double-edged sword. On the one hand, it enhanced the popularity of rhythm and blues, which was profitable for R & B artists and healthy

Rufus Thomas began his show-business career in Memphis as a deejay at WDIA, where he had a radio show from the 1940s through the mid-1970s. He is credited with orchestrating the talent shows that introduced B. B. King, Little Junior Parker, Bobby Blue Bland, and Issac Hayes.

A youthful B. B. King and Elvis Presley were captured backstage in Memphis in 1958 by African American photographer Ernest Withers, who has chronicled the Memphis music scene since the late 1940s. Cover versions of black songs by such early white rockers as Presley and Jerry Lee Lewis typically received more airplay than the originals.

for the music as a whole. But on the other hand, the "black roots, white fruits" syndrome was also at work here. White deejays were pushing into territory open to them due to the persistence of racial barriers in the radio industry, and they were doing so at the expense of the black disk jockeys, who continued to be barred from crossing over into the pop market. This racial dynamic also became evident once again in the music industry during the rise of rock-'n'-roll in the 1950s.

In its earliest manifestation, rock-'n'-roll was an innovative offshoot of rhythm and blues. The first wave of rock-'n'-rollers were all African American musicians who developed out of the postwar R & B milieu, the most important being Fats Domino, Little Richard, Bo Diddley, and Chuck Berry. Their music expressed a new urban sensibility that was especially attractive to both black and white teenagers. Given the proliferation of rhythm and blues through independent record labels and disk jockeys during this period, it was little wonder that white musicians such as Elvis Presley,

Bill Haley, Jerry Lee Lewis, and Buddy Holly began to copy the new black musical styles they heard all around them. And given the ongoing segregation in the music industry, it was also little wonder that their cover versions of popular black material received preferential treatment over the originals.

All too soon rock-'n'-roll became a big business—the large corporate labels bought up the white rockers and their music, while the independent record operations fell by the wayside. Elvis Presley signed a lucrative contract with RCA Victor, and Sun Records slowly went out of business a few years afterward.

Within the radio industry, the payola scandals of the late 1950s marked the end of an era in broadcasting. The power of the independent disk jockeys, both white and black, to play records of their own choosing was drastically curtailed with the subsequent rise of "top-40" formats. These formats institutionalized management's control over radio playlists, which determined which disks were to be heard on the airways. From the inception, top-40 formats tended to accelerate the music industry's growing hegemony over rock-'n'-roll.

At the end of the decade, the R & B-influenced rock-'n'-roll of Chuck Berry, Little Richard, Fats Domino, Jerry Lee Lewis, and the early Elvis Presley was giving way to the sanitized "schlock rock" of Fabian, Paul Anka, Frankie Avalon, and Pat Boone. Conventional pop and rock-'n'-roll were becoming virtually indistinguishable, while rhythm and blues was moving in an entirely new direction.

LOUIS JORDAN

The founding father of rhythm and blues was bandleader, vocalist, alto saxophonist, and songwriter Louis Jordan. In the late 1930s, he single-handedly pioneered the development of "jump blues" combos, which in turn supplanted the larger swing bands as the most popular black music ensembles of the day. His use of a scaled-down swing-band horn unit in conjunction with a four-piece rhythm section set the standard for rhythm-and-blues bands for years to come. In addition, Jordan's diverse repertoire of urban blues, swing-band dance numbers, hipster jive songs, and folksy novelty tunes significantly expanded the scope of musical resources and traditions available to up-and-coming R & B musicians in the postwar years.

In spite of these trailblazing achievements, Jordan is still best remembered and revered for his comic stage persona, which he cultivated during his early career in vaudeville and swing. The persona was that of a fun-loving and flamboyant black urban showman; it drew inspiration from both the sophisticated hipster humor of Cab Calloway and the down-home folk humor of Bert Williams. In fact, after he formed his own group, Louis Jordan billed himself as the "Modern Bert Williams" for a while, and on many occasions, he told the press that his goal as

an entertainer was to perform for millions of black people, not just a few "hepcats."

Louis Jordan was born in Brinkley, Arkansas, on July 8, 1908. His father was a professional musician and teacher who began to train his son on the clarinet at the age of seven. By the time he was a teenager, young Louis was also playing professionally in various local dance bands. After earning a degree in music from Arkansas Baptist College, he embarked on a career as a musician and performer. Jordan's first full-time job in the black entertainment industry was as a clarinetist

(Page 109) Louis Jordan is shown in a film still from *The Swing Parade of 1946*. (Right) Rhythm-and-blues pioneer Louis Jordan was a talented vocalist and musician whose material ranged from swing to urban blues to hipster jive numbers. Despite his pivotal contributions to the development of R & B, he is perhaps best remembered for such folksy novelty numbers as "That Chick's Too Young to Fry."

and dancer with the legendary Rabbit Foot Minstrels in the late 1920s. He also worked for vaudeville blues diva Ma Rainey's touring show.

In the early 1930s, Louis Jordan was based in Philadelphia, where he played for Charlie Gaines' swing band. He moved on to New York City in the mid-1930s to join Chick Webb's orchestra at the Savoy Ballroom. By this time, Jordan's instrument of choice was the alto saxophone. He remained with the Chick Webb orchestra until the bandleader's death in 1938. During this period, he played alto saxophone in the reed section, acted as the band's master of ceremonies, and handled the vocals on most of the novelty songs—thus sharing the limelight with Ella Fitzgerald.

After Chick Webb died, Jordan organized and led a nine-member house band at the Elks Rendezvous in New York City; within a year, he had trimmed his combo down to six musicians and named it "Louis Jordan and His Tympany Five" for a Decca recording session. Jordan remained with the Decca label for almost 15 years, from 1939 to 1953; they proved to be his most successful as a recording artist. His range of material, some of which he had a hand in writing, was nothing less than remarkable: swing classics such as "Choo Choo Ch' Boogie," urban blues such as "I'm Gonna Move to the Outskirts of Town," hipster jive numbers such as "Reet Petite and Gone," and especially the folksy novelty songs such as "That Chick's Too Young to Fry," "Beans and Cornbread," and "Somebody Done Changed the Lock on My Door."

Louis Jordan's first records to make the race charts in the early 1940s were "What's the Use of Getting Sober?" and "Five Guys Named Moe." His first hit to cross over onto the pop charts was the 1946 novelty number "Caldonia," which was covered by Woody Herman for the occasion. Jordan's other major R & B hits in the postwar era included "Saturday Night Fish Fry," a hilarious cautionary tale of black urban life; "Ain't Nobody Here But Us Chickens," a tongue-in-check spoof of black rural life; and "Let the Good Times Roll," which became the unofficial anthem of the rhythm-and-blues generation.

During the height of his career in the postwar years, Louis Jordan was a towering figure in black popular music. In addition to his recordings, concerts, and club dates, he was involved in a number of Hollywood films and appeared on network radio and television. By the early 1950s, his popularity was peaking, and a younger generation of R & B musicians was on the rise. Many of them, such as Chuck Berry and Bill Haley, who also recorded for Decca, borrowed freely and frequently from Jordan's style and repertoire; but while they went on to rock-'n'-roll stardom, their mentor's career leveled off. Even though he inspired the rock-'n'-roll revolution, Louis Jordan was not able to capitalize on it. Nevertheless, he remained active in rhythm-and-blues circles up until his death in 1974. More recently, he received some long-overdue recognition when he was posthumously inducted into the Rock-'n'-Roll Hall of Fame.

NAT KING COLE

By far the most successful African American recording artist of the postwar era was Nat King Cole. From the time he recorded his first hit record in 1944 up until his death in 1965, he was reputed to have sold 50 million records for the Capitol label; the profits generated by the sale of these disks transformed Capitol into a major record company. At the height of his popularity in the 1950s, Nat King Cole joined pop music icons Frank Sinatra, Bing Crosby, and Perry Como at the pinnacle of the record industry, and like them, he became a millionaire. But unlike Sinatra, Crosby, and Como, Nat King Cole owed his fame and fortune almost exclusively to the sale of records. In Cole's case at least, crossing over onto the pop music charts proved much easier than doing so in film and television.

Like Sam Cooke, Nathaniel Adams Cole was the Chicago-raised son of a southern Baptist minister. He was born in Montgomery, Alabama, in 1919 and moved with his family to Chicago's Southside black community five years later. His mother taught him how to play the piano, and later, he received professional training, also on the keyboards. While still in his teens, Nat King Cole played piano in a number of local jazz combos; for a period in the mid-1930s, he also worked as the pianist in the vaudeville show band traveling with the black musical "Shuffle Along."

After the company disbanded in Los Angeles in 1937, Cole remained in the city to work in some of the local nightclubs. When the manager of one of these jazz clubs suggested that he form his own group for an extended engagement, the Nat King Cole Trio was born. At this point in his career, Cole was a promising jazz pianist who would occasionally sing a standard tune if asked to do so by a patron. Then in 1943, the fledgling Capitol label signed the trio to a contract; their first release was a vocal number by Nat King Cole called "Straighten Up and Fly Right," which was based on a sermon his father once delivered. The record sold a half-million copies. It was the first R & B hit for the new record company, and it launched Cole's career as a vocalist.

Nat King Cole had even greater success with his recording of "Christmas Song" in 1945. Then after the 1946 release of "Nature Boy," his trio broke up, and Cole became a solo artist. In 1949, his recording of "Mona Lisa" crossed over onto the pop charts. It eventually sold three million copies and established him as the best-selling African American recording artist of his generation.

During the 1950s, Nat King Cole extended his string of hits on the pop charts with "Too Young," "A Fool Was I," "Answer Me, My Love," "A Blossom Fell," and "Time and the River." In addition, he appeared in two Hollywood films, "The Blue Gardenia" in 1952, and "Saint Louis Blues," a biography of W. C. Handy, in 1958. It was also during this period that he hosted a weekly 15-minute variety show for NBC. As it turned out, however, even though the program had respectable ratings, Cole was unable to continue the series beyond a year. Advertisers were afraid to sponsor an African

(Page 113) The Nat King Cole Trio gained gradual popularity while playing in small nightclubs in Hollywood and New York in the early 1940s. (Right) Nat King Cole was an international star by the early 1950s, making occasional concert tours to South America, Australia, and the Caribbean. He was also a featured actor and performer in film, television, and radio. In 1956-1957, Cole was the only African American to have his own variety show on network television.

American on network television because they feared hostile southern markets and the possibility of a nationwide boycott of their products if they became stereotyped as "Negro" merchandise. The experience was a painful one for Cole, and he never hosted another television show.

Nat King Cole continued to add to his string of pop hits for Capitol and appeared in one final film—"Cat Ballou"—before he succumbed to lung cancer in 1965. His last million-selling single was, appropriately, "Unforgettable," which was released within a year of his death. His loss signaled the end of an age in black popular music. He was the last of the great swing-era crooners to consistently break into the pop charts in the postwar years. After Nat King Cole, the style had no outstanding champion. In fact, it wasn't until the 1992 release of the critically acclaimed album, "Unforgettable," by his daughter, Natalie Cole, that the stylistic genius of her father re-emerged—literally. With the aid of multitrack digital recording equipment, the daughter sang a duet with her father on "Unforgettable." Subsequently, the number was awarded a Grammy for pop song of the year.

DINAH WASHINGTON

Dinah Washington was born Ruth Lee Jones in Tuscaloosa, Alabama, in 1924. At the age of four, young Ruth and her family joined the thousands of African Americans who were making the great exodus north in search of a better life. They settled on Chicago's Southside in 1931. As a youngster, Ruth was give the nickname "Alligator" because of her bad complexion; she was also often teased about being overweight. Both conditions would plague her for the rest of her life.

Her father, Ollie Jones, was a habitual gambler who abandoned his family soon after arriving in Chicago. Her mother, Alice Williams, was a devout member of a local church; she taught her daughter to sing gospel and involved her in the church choir. When she was 16, Ruth Jones caught the eye of gospel legend Sallie Martin; she joined Martin's all-female gospel entourage as the pianist and later vocalist, accompanying them on national tours.

In the early 1940s, Ruth Jones left Sallie Martin's group, married her first husband, and began to sing urban blues and swing jazz in the Southside's clubs and bars. During this period, Billie Holiday often appeared in Chicago; Ruth would attend every evening performance to soak up Billie's style and song repertoire. In 1943, Joe Glaser heard Ruth Jones sing in a Southside nightclub and signed her as the female vocalist with the Lionel Hampton band, which he managed. It was around this time that she was also given the name Dinah Washington to help launch her new career, credit for which was claimed by Hampton, among others.

In December 1943, Dinah Washington made her first appearance at Harlem's Apollo Theater. Music critic and songwriter Leonard Feather was in the audience, and seeing her potential as a blues singer, he arranged for her first recording session with Keynote Records. Two of the releases, "Evil Gal Blues" and "Salty Papa Blues," both penned by Feather, were successful enough to establish Dinah as an up-and-coming R & B female vocalist. Over the next few years, she continued to record and perform for a growing audience.

Although her voice and style were most evocative of the blues, Dinah was a very versatile singer. She could fill a song with a full range of emotions and convey the highs and lows of intense feelings to her listeners. She had perfect diction, which may have come in part from watching Bette Davis movies, one of her favorite pastimes as a young girl. While she had a strong voice with a distinctive timbre, Dinah Washington never sang a song the same way twice.

Dinah's 15-year career with Chicago-based Mercury Records proved to be her most successful

(Page 115) Blues vocalist Dinah Washington poses for an ad promoting her appearance at Birdland in New York City in 1958. (Right) This is an early publicity photograph of Dinah Washington, made in 1943 when she was touring with Lionel Hampton and His Band.

period as a recording artist. She signed with the label in 1946 and initially recorded black cover versions of white pop songs. Then the label began to utilize her more as a blues vocalist, and she was crowned "Queen of the Blues" by its publicity department. In 1949, her "Baby Get Lost" made it to the top of the R & B charts; in 1952, her "Trouble in Mind" climbed to the number-four position on the same charts. Her biggest hit was "What a Difference a Day Makes," which crossed over onto the pop charts' top-ten listings from its number-one position on the R & B charts and won her a Grammy for best rhythm-and-blues recording of 1959.

When she wasn't recording, Dinah maintained a busy touring schedule. Like many African American performers of her time, she faced humiliation and discrimination in the South and resented her second-class citizenship. In response, she was a strong supporter and personal friend of Dr. Martin Luther King, Jr., often doing benefits for his civil rights projects.

Dinah enjoyed a great camaraderie with her fellow musicians, who were mostly men. Two of her seven husbands were musicians she worked with regularly, drummer Jimmy Cobb and saxophonist Eddie Chamblee. Her innate ability to surround herself with first-rate musicians enhanced her range as an artist.

Over the years, she sang with trios, big bands, bebop groups, R & B combos, and string sections. The list of jazz luminaries she performed with included saxophonists Arnett Cobb and Cannonball Adderly, pianist Junior Mance, vibraphonist Milt Jackson, bass player Charles Mingus, trumpeter Clark Terry, and the Count Basie orchestra, to name but a few.

Unfortunately, the loneliness and insecurities of Dinah's childhood affected the way she interacted with people throughout her life. She constantly surrounded herself with friends, family, and musicians. She was very generous with her time and money, loved to cook southern soul food, and was renowned for the late-night house parties she held in her Harlem apartment. She was admired by both the black gay community and the southern migrants. But when Dinah commanded the center of attention, she could often be insulting to other women whom she perceived as threats. She was spunky and quick-witted, and her short temper led to many arguments and even physical fights.

Toward the end of Dinah Washington's career, she began missing her club engagements and acting rudely toward her audience. Because of her ongoing battle with excessive weight, she started taking prescription drugs for weight loss, then other drugs including sleeping pills. By 1960, she was also taking mercury injections to induce weight loss through dehydration. Along with her heavy drinking, the prescription drugs and mercury finally took their toll. Dinah Washington died of an overdose of sleeping pills, diet pills, and alcohol on December 11, 1963.

SAM COOKE

In spite of the brevity of his career as a secular recording artist, Sam Cooke was a pivotal figure in black popular music throughout the 1950s and the early 1960s. He brought the emotional flavor and feel of gospel into rhythm and blues, thereby setting the stage for the emergence of soul music. More than any other African American vocalist of his generation, he bridged the gap between the urban blues and swing crooners of the postwar era, such as Nat King Cole, Charles Brown, Joe Williams, and Billy Eckstine, and the poignant soul balladeers of the 1960s, such as Otis Redding, Sam and Dave, Jackie Wilson, Jerry Butler, and Curtis Mayfield.

In addition, Sam Cooke was the first major sex symbol—however sublimated—of the gospel movement's golden age, and he brought his good looks and charisma with him when he crossed over to become a rhythm-and-blues singer. During the late 1950s and early 1960s, Cooke was by far the most popular male vocalist in black music, but his meteoric career was cut short in 1964, when he was shot in a Los Angeles motel by a night clerk under unusual circumstances. His loss would prove to be a significant one for the future of rhythm and blues.

Sam Cooke was born in Clarksdale, Mississippi, in 1931. He was one of eight sons of a local Baptist preacher, who migrated to Chicago with his family in the late 1930s. At the time, Chicago's Southside was a mecca for black gospel music—Thomas Dorsey, Sallie Martin, Mahalia Jackson,

Roberta Martin, and the Soul Stirrers were all active there. Young Sam's first gospel experience came when he and three of his brothers formed a quartet called the Singing Children. By the time he entered high school, Cooke was singing with the Highway O Cs, the Southside's most important teenage gospel group. In 1949, at the age of 18, Sam Cooke replaced R. H. Harris as the lead singer in the Soul Stirrers, perhaps the most famous modern gospel quartet in the country.

Over the next eight years, Cooke was a star attraction on the gospel circuit; his emotional falsetto phrasing electrified black churchgoers throughout the land and won for him a large and loyal following. During this period, he made his most memorable gospel recordings with the Soul Stirrers; they included "Touch the Hem of His Garment," "Nearer to Thee," and "Jesus Wash away My Troubles."

Sam Cooke's celebrated crossover to rhythm and blues created a major controversy in black music circles, both sacred and secular. Many of his African American gospel fans were so offended that they totally disassociated themselves from him and his new musical career. Specialty's owner, Art Rupee, refused to market Cooke as a rhythm-and-blues artist. It was only when he scored his first big hit with "You Send Me" on a competing label in 1957 that Rupee agreed to support Sam Cooke's crossover aspirations.

After a few years with Specialty, Cooke signed a million-dollar contract with RCA Victor, which also gave him complete control over the artistic decisions involved in his recording activities on the label. He was able to compose and record some of his best material for RCA Victor, in particular "Twisting the Night Away," "Bring It on Home to Me," and "A Change Is Gonna Come." All of these songs made it to the top of the R & B charts.

The final years of Sam Cooke's life were marked with triumph and tragedy. He achieved national stardom, became a millionaire, and found some measure of personal happiness when he married his high-school sweetheart, Barbara Campbell, in 1960. A year after the wedding, she gave birth to Sam's first son, Vincent. A year and a half later, the boy drowned in the family swimming pool. Despite his grief, Cooke continued with his rigorous touring and recording schedule, and there was even talk of his forming an independent record company.

As had been the case throughout his career, he was attracting legions of female fans wherever he appeared, and as it turned out, this adulation proved to be Sam Cooke's Achilles' heel. On the night that he was shot, he had picked up a woman after his final show and taken her to a three-dollar-a-night Los Angeles motel. The woman entered the rented room with him, but soon thereafter fled with some of his clothing, later claiming that he had become abusive. When the partially clothed Cooke appeared unarmed, but possibly agitated, at the motel office, he was beaten with a club and

then shot dead by the white female night clerk. She testified that Cooke had tried to assault her, and the death was ruled to be justifiable homicide, but rumors of foul play persisted for years.

More than 25,000 mourners attended Sam Cooke's funeral rites at the Tabernacle Baptist Church in Chicago; Ray Charles was the featured vocalist. A few weeks after his death, "A Change Is Gonna Come" was released by RCA Victor, and the record went right to the top of the R & B charts. Almost overnight, the song became a rallying cry for the civil rights movement, and Sam Cooke became one of its fallen heroes.

This publicity shot of Sam Cooke was taken early in his solo career. His controversial crossover to rhythm and blues lost him legions of African American gospel fans. Written as a tribute to the national dance craze, Cooke's "Twistin' the Night Away" became a hit in 1962.

119

Conclusion
THE EMERGENCE OF SOUL

The emergence in the 1960s of the African American popular music known as "soul" was the high-water mark in the development of rhythm and blues. The dominant R & B innovators during this period continued to experiment with various combinations of urban blues, gospel, and jazz, but, in addition, new technological and commercial considerations were coming into play. Among them were multitrack recording studios, FM radio stations, transistor radio receivers, corporate distribution deals, and crossover marketing strategies. The unprecedented success of Barry Gordy at Motown Records in Detroit brought many of these new tendencies in black popular music to the forefront.

Gordy founded Motown in the early 1960s with the idea of using it as a vehicle for integrating the pop record charts. Working with local musicians in his own recording studio, he developed an assembly-line technique aimed at maximum crossover. The famous "Motown sound" featured a strong and always-present bass line, lush string and horn arrangements, and upbeat lyrics. It was an irresistibly danceable music that was appealing to both black and white teenagers, much like rock-'n'-roll a decade earlier.

Moreover, Motown's music factory, named "Hitsville USA," mass-produced songs that were especially tailored for airplay on AM radio stations with top-40 formats. As a result, most of its impressive string of pop hits during the 1960s were less than three minutes in length, and, invariably,

they featured youthful lead singers whose vocals stood out in the higher treble audio frequencies so prominent in AM radio reception. For example, Smokey Robinson, Little Stevie Wonder, Diana Ross, and Michael Jackson all had voices that were well suited for AM airplay.

Barry Gordy not only created a hit-record factory in Detroit's black ghetto, he also built from the ground up the largest African American music corporation in the entire country. To accomplish this amazing feat, Gordy relied on the vertical integration of all facets of his company's operations. This included top-down control of production and distribution as well as songwriting, publishing, publicity, tour bookings, artist development, personal management, and even etiquette. Motown not only had its own record promoters, booking agents, songwriting teams, record producers, studio musicians, and recording artists, but also its own choreographers, fashion designers, and even a "charm school" for its female acts.

This detailed approach to organization paid big dividends. And to his credit, Gordy relied heavily on local black talent, which he then groomed for the long commerical haul; he did not simply exploit his artists for one or two hits songs, a practice all too common with R & B performers in the 1950s. As a consequence, original Motown acts such as the Miracles, the Temptations, the Four Tops, and the Supremes enjoyed a longevity that was unheard of for most African American entertainers in the pop market.

The "Godfather of Soul," James Brown formed his first group, the Famous Flames, in Macon, Georgia, in 1954. By 1956, he had a hit record, "Please, Please, Please." He rose to stardom in the 1960s with such singles as "Prisoner of Love," "Mashed Potatoes," and "Say It Loud (I'm Black and I'm Proud)."

Soul great Aretha Franklin received her training as a gospel singer and pianist in the early 1950s from family friends and gospel legends Mahalia Jackson, the Clara Ward Singers, and the Reverend James Cleveland. In 1960, she was encouraged to lead a career in secular music by Sam Cooke, who himself began as a gospel singer.

At first, Motown was a progressive force in the music industry. The company pioneered career development for popular black artists, and it fashioned the most sustained crossover strategy of the 1960s. In the process, however, its formula for success became reified. The centralized control and discipline once seemingly necessary for survival in a cutthroat business environment eventually became oppressive to many of Motown's leading recording artists, tunesmiths, and record producers. As the corporation expanded and its employees matured, a number of them came to resent Gordy's total control over their careers and, to a certain extent, even their lives.

Money also became a divisive issue, especially since Gordy owned all of Motown's stock and thus pocketed a lion's share of the profits. Soon there were numerous defections in the ranks, and the company lost its edge in the pop music market. Gordy then moved the corporation to Hollywood and eventually sold it to MCA. Nevertheless, many of Motown's more talented artists were able to overcome its oppressive organizational constraints and mature into compelling composers and performers in their own right. Among the most distinguished Motown alumni were Stevie Wonder, Marvin Gaye, Smokey Robinson, Diana Ross, and Michael Jackson. Collectively, these artists helped to shape and define soul music throughout the 1960s and beyond.

The other major center associated with the rise of soul music was located in the Mid South, where a small number of key independent record companies and recording studios were based in the 1960s. The rhythm and blues produced by these operations borrowed freely from the urban blues, gospel, and jazz traditions, but it was above all else a vocal art form.

Like the blues, it had a compelling social message. However, the emotional fervor of the vocal line was its defining characteristic, and that was taken from the gospel tradition. Secular love and salvation superseded the sacred themes in these gospel songs, but the song structures, emotional expressiveness, and the rhythms remained the same. The vocal line was then further embellished by a jazzy horn section playing call-and-response riffs. A rhythm section rounded out the sound by laying down the required groundbeat and bass patterns; it included drums, electric bass, rhythm guitar, and sometimes an electric piano or organ. The net result was an enticing mix of propulsive rhythms, sonorous instrumental solos, and impassioned vocals.

The Mid South's two leading recording operations were located in Memphis, Tennessee, and Muscle Shoals, Alabama. Most of the activity in Memphis revolved around the Stax/Volt labels, which from 1963 to 1975 went through one of the most spectacular boom-and-bust cycles in the history of the music industry. The venture began as a neighborhood recording studio in the city's black ghetto, which employed a handful of young local musicians, black and white, to make a series of recordings for a regional audience. It quickly mushroomed into a multimillion-dollar music enterprise with more than 50 acts on its roster. At its zenith in the late 1960s, Stax/Volt was making $14 million annually, rivaling Motown as the nation's most successful African American record company.

The labels' rosters included home-grown products such as Rufus and Carla Thomas, Booker T. and the MGs, and Isaac Hayes. But it was the out-of-town performers that the labels recorded, especially Sam and Dave and Otis Redding, who had the greatest appeal and impact on the direction of soul music in the 1960s. Redding in particular was a prodigious talent destined for greatness until his death in a plane crash late in 1967. From that point on, the Stax/Volt operation fell on hard times, and it eventually went bankrupt.

The Fame recording studio in Muscle Shoals, Alabama, was not as well known as the Stax/Volt studios in Memphis, but it proved to be just as important for the development of soul music. The studio was a cooperative venture undertaken by a small group of young local musicians and songwriters—all of whom were white males. They had grown up listening to rhythm and blues on WLAC, and by the time they established their studio, they were devout students of the music. Significantly, they scored their greatest triumphs recording black soul vocalists. A few of these, such as Percy Sledge, were local products, but most, such as Joe Tex and Aretha Franklin, were brought in by outside labels.

The success of Sledge's "When a Man Loves a Woman" in 1966 attracted the attention of Atlantic Record's Jerry Wexler, who soon thereafter brought Wilson Picket and Aretha Franklin to the Fame studio for recording sessions. Franklin had just come over to Atlantic from Columbia Records, where producer John Hammond had attempted unsuccessfully to groom her as an urban blues singer in the Billie Holiday/Dinah Washington mold. For the Muscle Shoals sessions, Aretha Franklin returned to her gospel roots. The result was a remarkable series of recordings that would make her the most popular female soul vocalist of the decade.

Aretha Franklin's male counterpart in soul music during the 1960s was James Brown. Both started their musical careers as gospel singers, a background that helps to account for the fervent vocal style they employed in their music and for Brown's frenzied performance rituals. His live shows, complete with a large orchestra, back-up singers and dancers, and his personal master of ceremonies, were legendary on the chitlin circuit and made him into a folk hero for African Americans. In 1962, an album of his stage show, "Live at the Apollo," crossed over onto the pop charts, sold in the millions, and became one of the most acclaimed releases of the decade.

Brown was at the center of two major musical innovations during this period. One was to extend the rhythmic dimensions of a song until they totally dominated it. The bass lines and patterns came to the forefront of the music, and the

The Apollo Theater has remained an institution in African American popular entertainment for more than 50 years. From jazz to blues to bebop to gospel to soul, the Apollo is responsible for ushering in the careers of many well-known African American performers.

rhythm section became, in effect, a lead instrument. In this respect, Brown was a precursor of the funk bands of the 1970s. His second innovation was to engage the audience in sermonlike storytelling, which anticipated the advent of rap and hip-hop music by more than a decade. The song, "Say It Loud, I'm Black and I'm Proud" was indicative of this sermonizing tendency. Along with Aretha Franklin's version of Otis Redding's "Respect," "Say It Loud" became a clarion call for the civil rights struggles of the 1960s.

Soul music was the culmination of the rhythm-and-blues tradition. It brought together all of the key elements from urban blues, gospel, and swing even as it laid the groundwork for a radical transformation of these traditions. As such, it bridged the gap between postwar rhythm and blues

and postmodern hip-hop. Moreover, soul music was organically linked to the tenor of the times; it was the secular music of the civil rights movement, the ghetto uprisings, the antiwar movement, and the black power movement. When these struggles died out in the 1970s, the message in the music lost its cutting edge.

Nevertheless, the soul legacy is an exceptional one in the history of African American popular music. Not only did soul musicians provide continuity with the past by mining the mother lode of rhythm-and-blues traditions, but they also reworked those traditions into a new genre of black popular song. And even though that musical genre was short lived, it continues to resonate in the present-day trends in popular music, both black and white.

SELECT BIBLIOGRAPHY

Barlow, William. *Looking Up at Down: The Emergence of Blues Culture*. Philadelphia: Temple University Press, 1989.

Collier, James Lincoln. *Duke Ellington*. New York: Oxford University Press, 1987.

Collier, James Lincoln. *The Making of Jazz: A Comprehensive History*. New York: Oxford University Press, 1978.

Dance, Helen Oakley. *Stormy Monday: The T-Bone Walker Story*. Baton Rouge: Louisiana State University Press, 1987.

Dance, Stanley. *The World of Count Basie*. New York: Da Capo Press, Inc., 1980.

Dates, Jannette and William Barlow. *Split Image: African Americans in the Mass Media*. 2nd Ed. Washington, D.C.: Howard University Press, 1993.

Ewen, David. *All The Years of American Popular Music*. Englewood Cliffs, N. J.: Prentice-Hall, 1977.

Fernett, Gene. *Swing Out! Great Negro Dance Bands*. Midland, Mich.: Pendell Publishing Company, 1970.

Gitler, Ira. *Jazz Masters of the Forties*. New York: Collier Books, 1966.

Haskins, Jim. *Queen of the Blues: A Biography of Dinah Washington*. New York: Wiliam Morrow and Company, 1987.

Hirshey, Gerri. *Nowhere to Run: The Story of Soul Music*. London: Penguin Books, 1985.

Holiday, Billie and William Dufty. *Lady Sings the Blues*. New York: Doubleday & Company, 1956.

McCarthy, Albert. *Big Band Jazz*. New York: Berkeley Publishing Company, 1974.

Russell, Ross. *Jazz Style in Kansas City and the Southwest*. Berkeley: University of California Press, 1971.

Shaw, Arnold. *Honkers and Shouters: The Golden Years of Rhythm and Blues*. New York: Collier Books, 1978.

Vance, Joel. *Fats Waller: His Life and Times*. New York: Berkeley Publishing Company, 1977.

INDEX

129

ILLUSTRATION AND PHOTO CREDITS

Every effort has been made to properly credit the illustrators and photographers represented in this volume. If any oversight has been made, please accept our sincerest apologies. The authors gratefully acknowledge the following contributions:

Endsheets: record labels courtesy of Hank O'Neal; **4**: © William P. Gottlieb; **7**: Courtesy of the Library of Congress, Farm Security Administration Collection; **8 and 10**: © MICHAEL OCHS ARCHIVES/Venice, Ca.; **11, 12,** and **13**: Courtesy of the Library of Congress, Farm Security Administration Collection; **14**: Photograph by Berenice Abbott, © Commerce Graphics Ltd., Inc.; **15**: © MICHAEL OCHS ARCHIVES/Venice, Ca.; **16**: Courtesy of Pete Whelan, "78 Quarterly"; **17** and **18**: Frank Driggs Collection; **19**: © MICHAEL OCHS ARCHIVES/Venice, Ca.; **20**: © William Claxton; **21**: Courtesy of the Library of Congress, Farm Security Administration Collection; **23**: Courtesy of Helen Oakley Dance; **25**: © Stephen C. LaVere; **29**: photographs by the Hooks Brothers, © MICHAEL OCHS ARCHIVES/ Memphis Music & Blues Museum; **33**: Courtesy of Helen Oakley Dance; **34**: © MICHAEL OCHS ARCHIVES/Venice, Ca.; **36**: Frank Driggs Collection; **40**: © MICHAEL OCHS ARCHIVES/Venice, Ca.; **41**: © Morgan & Marvin Smith, courtesy of the Photographs and Prints Division, Schomburg Center for Research in Black Culture, The New York Public Library; **43**: Courtesy of the Museum of Modern Art, Film Stills Archive; **45**: Frank Driggs Collection; **46, 48,** and **51**: © MICHAEL OCHS ARCHIVES/Venice, Ca.; **52** and **55**: Frank Driggs Collection; **57**: Courtesy of the Manuscripts Division, Schomburg Center for Research in Black Culture, The New York Public Library; **58**: Courtesy of Department of Special Collections, Boston University; **59**: Photograph by Serge Balkin, courtesy of Tom Caravaglia; **62**: © Austin Hansen, courtesy of the Photographs and Prints Division, Schomburg Center for Research in Black Culture, The New York Public Library; **66, 67,** and **68**: Frank Driggs Collection; **71**: © William P. Gottlieb; **72**: Frank Driggs Collection; **73**: © William P. Gottlieb; **74**: © William Claxton; **75**: © William P. Gottlieb; **81**: Frank Driggs Collection; **83**: © MICHAEL OCHS ARCHIVES/Venice, Ca.; **86**: © Esther Bubley; **90**: © 1991 Alice Ochs/MICHAEL OCHS ARCHIVES/Venice, Ca.; **94, 97, 98, 101, 102, 103,** and **105**: © MICHAEL OCHS ARCHIVES/Venice, Ca.; **106**: © Stephen C. LaVere; **107**: photographs by the Hooks Brothers, © MICHAEL OCHS ARCHIVES/ Memphis Music & Blues Museum; **108**: © Stephen C. LaVere; **110** and **114**: © MICHAEL OCHS ARCHIVES/Venice, Ca.; **116**: Frank Driggs Collection; **120**: © Kwame Brathwaite, courtesy of the Photographs and Prints Division, Schomburg Center for Research in Black Culture, The New York Public Library; **122**: © 1993 Frank Driggs/Michael Ochs Archives/Venice, Ca. **126**: Frank Driggs Collection.

The following contributions are courtesy of the Photographs and Prints Division, Schomburg Center for Research in Black Culture, The New York Public Library; 2, 22, (Jazz Museum Collection), 38, 42, 47, 49, 50, 53, 54, 61, 77, 78 (Jazz Museum Collection), 79, 80, 85, 87, 89, 92, 93, 95, 96, 109, 113, 115, 119, and 125.